Hearts

by

Patricia Burke

'Hearts' is published by coloradoodle Publications United States of America

*****

ISBN-10: 0-9975959-3-0
ISBN-13: 978-0-9975959-3-2

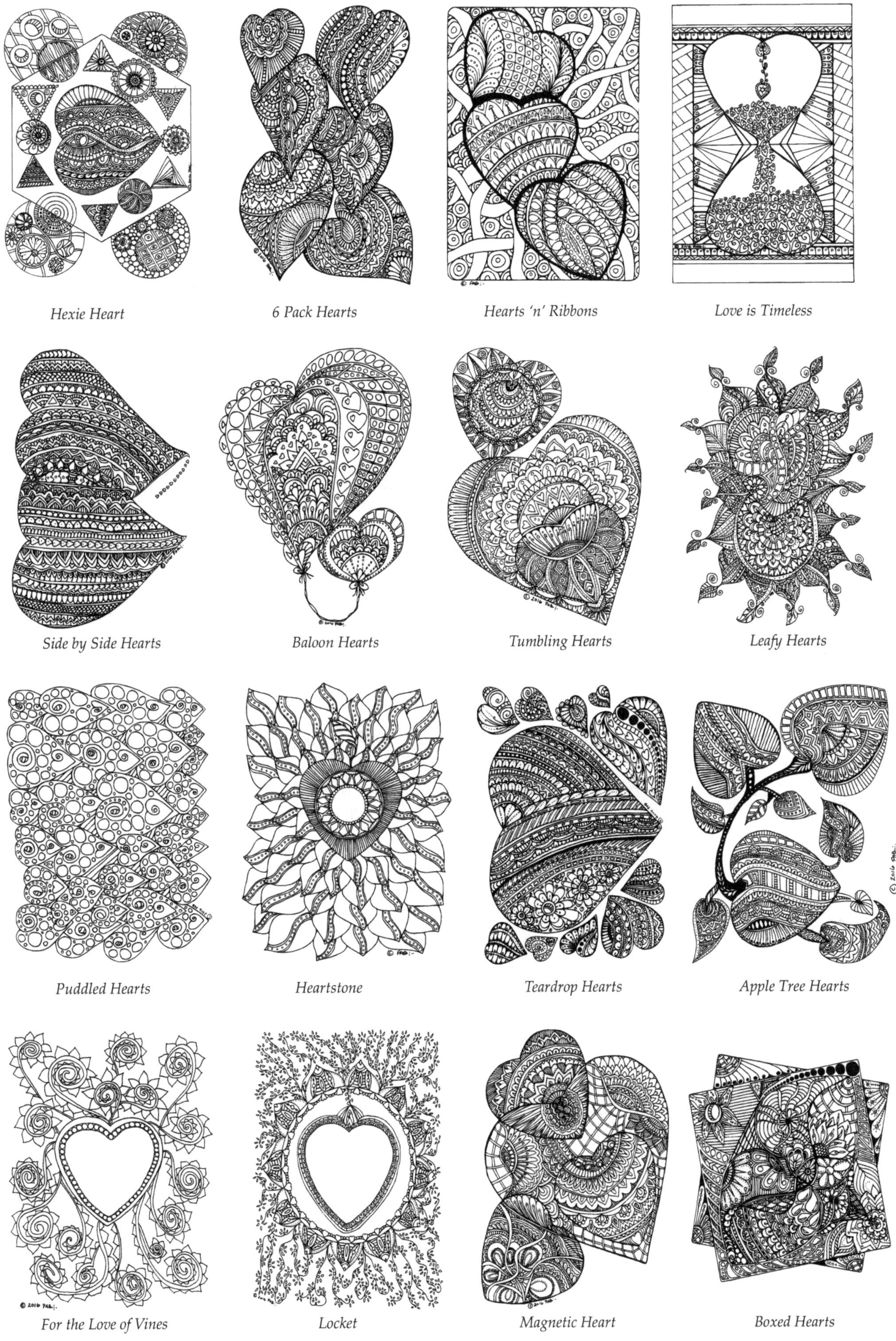

Hexie Heart · *6 Pack Hearts* · *Hearts 'n' Ribbons* · *Love is Timeless*

Side by Side Hearts · *Baloon Hearts* · *Tumbling Hearts* · *Leafy Hearts*

Puddled Hearts · *Heartstone* · *Teardrop Hearts* · *Apple Tree Hearts*

For the Love of Vines · *Locket* · *Magnetic Heart* · *Boxed Hearts*

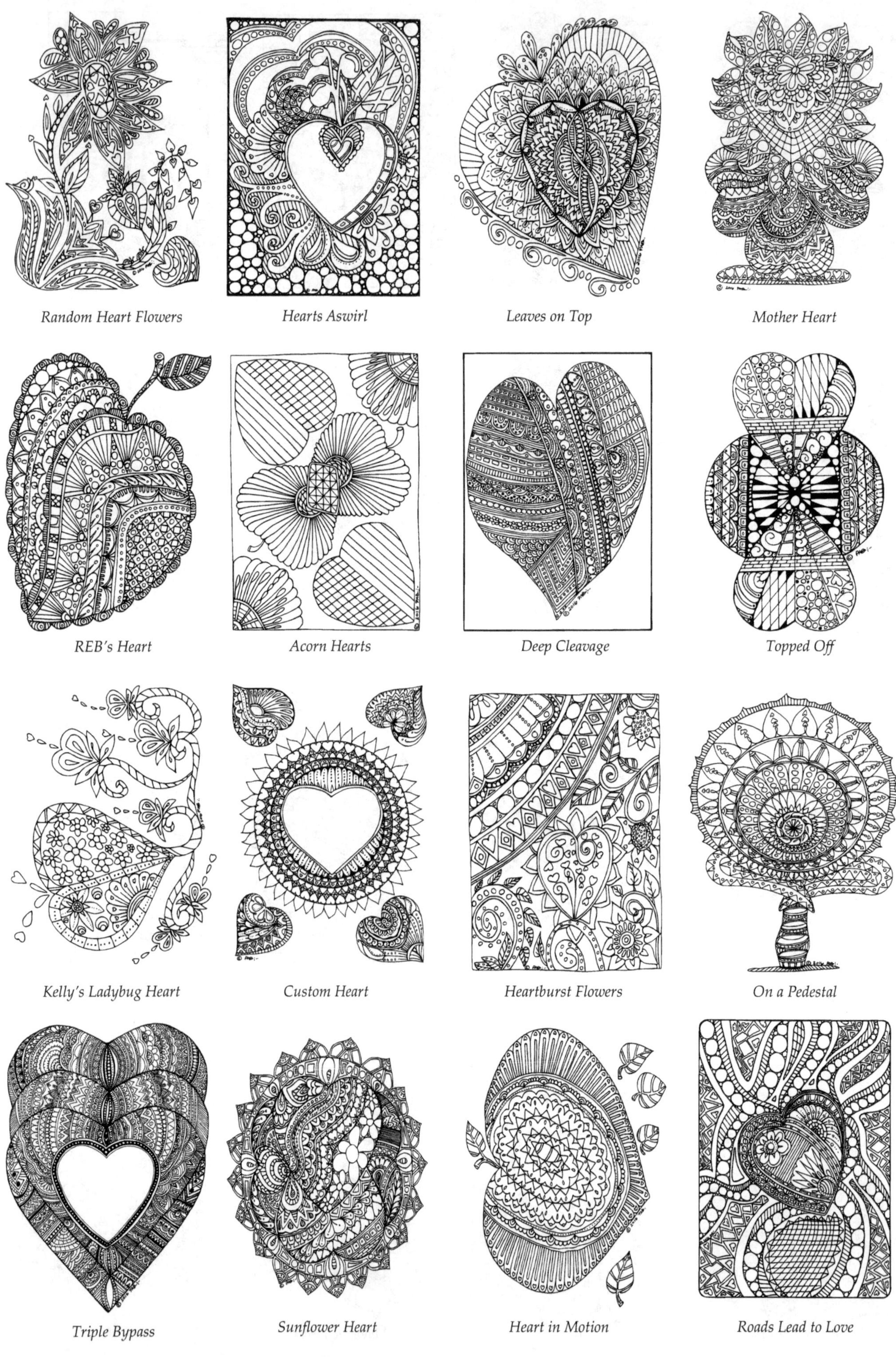

Random Heart Flowers — *Hearts Aswirl* — *Leaves on Top* — *Mother Heart*

REB's Heart — *Acorn Hearts* — *Deep Cleavage* — *Topped Off*

Kelly's Ladybug Heart — *Custom Heart* — *Heartburst Flowers* — *On a Pedestal*

Triple Bypass — *Sunflower Heart* — *Heart in Motion* — *Roads Lead to Love*

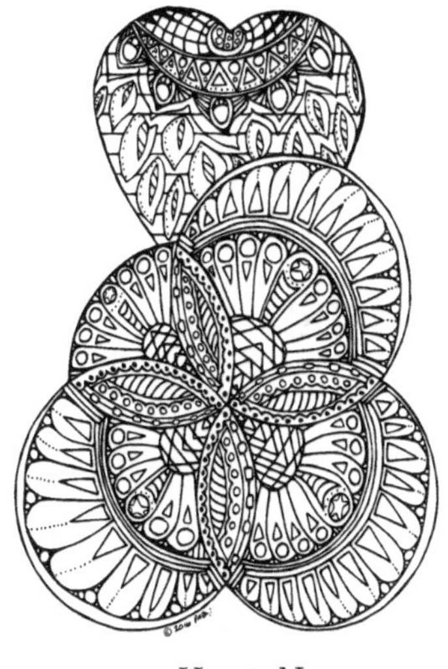

Hearts Up

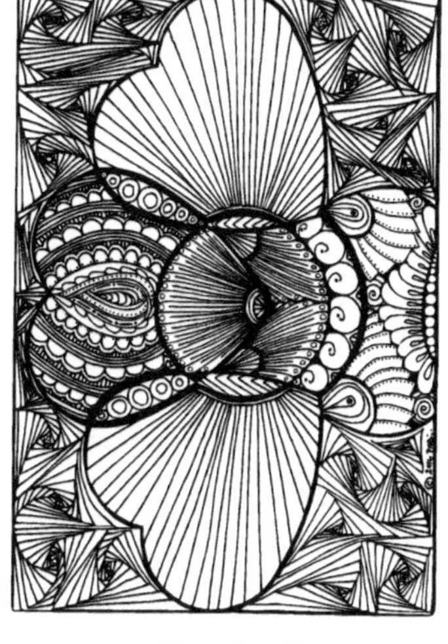

Emotional

Love Shoes? Please check out my book "SHOE-DLES" available on Amazon.Com. Everybody love shoes.

Also check out "ZOO-DLES" on Amazon, a fun-filled book of animals of all kinds in this awesome doodle style.

To REB...

After forty years,

you still hold the key to my heart.

* * * * *

~Cover Art Drawn and Doodled by ~

Patricia Burke

* * * * *

~Cover Art Colorist~

Lina Weikel

* * * * *

~Incredible Tech Support provided by~

Shelah Dow

* * * * *

My Fantastic Colorists

Corie Irvine
Debbie Mulkey
Elizabeth Herriott
Jennifer Knisley Preston
Kelly Deuber Taylor
Lina Weikel
Lisa Frey
Lynda Greer
Marian Radius
Shannon Woodford Schuler
Shawn Elliott
Shelah Dow

Thank you for your sharp eyes and amazing skill.
We have so much more to do.
{{Hugs}}

THIS BOOK BELONGS TO

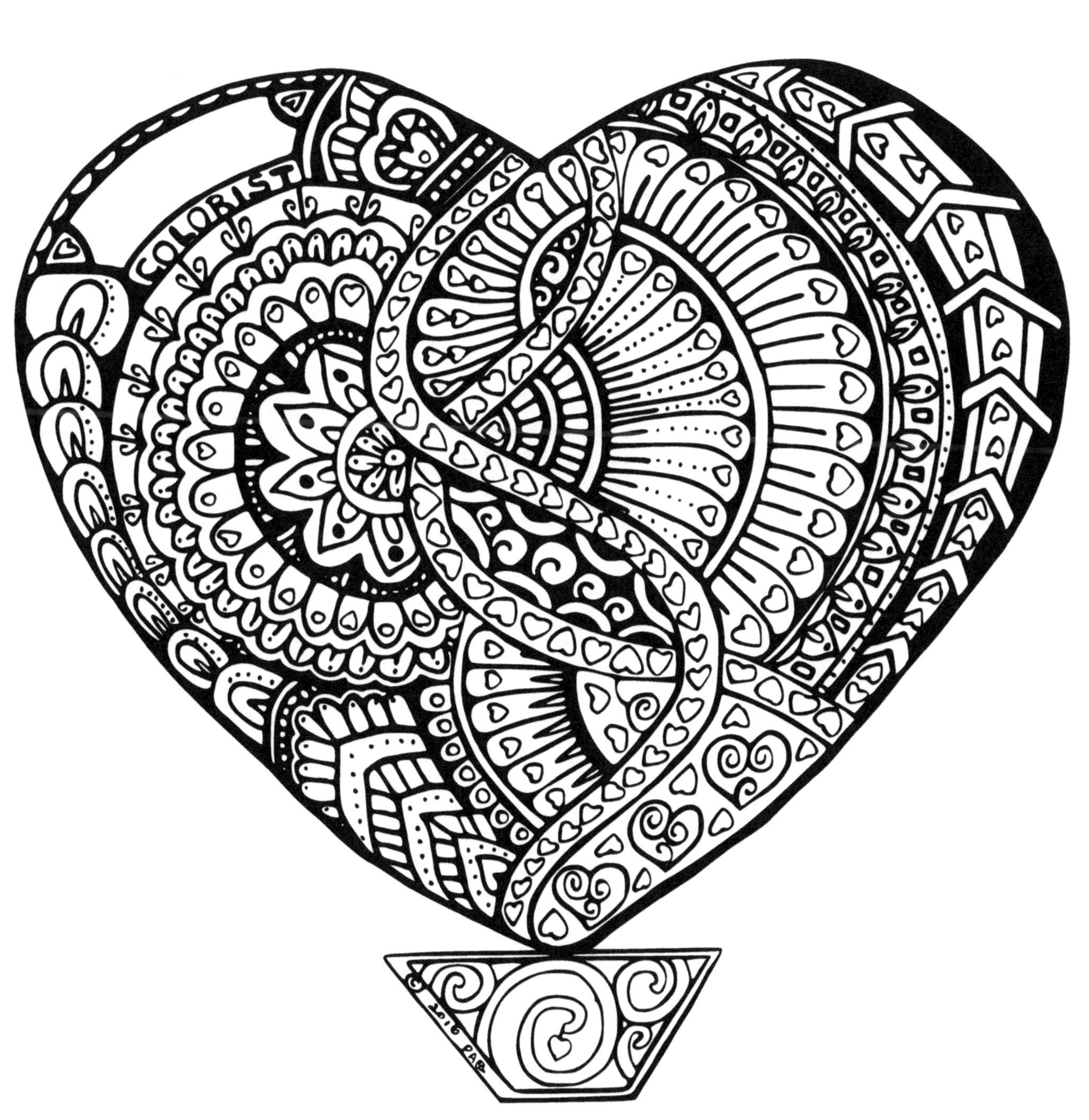

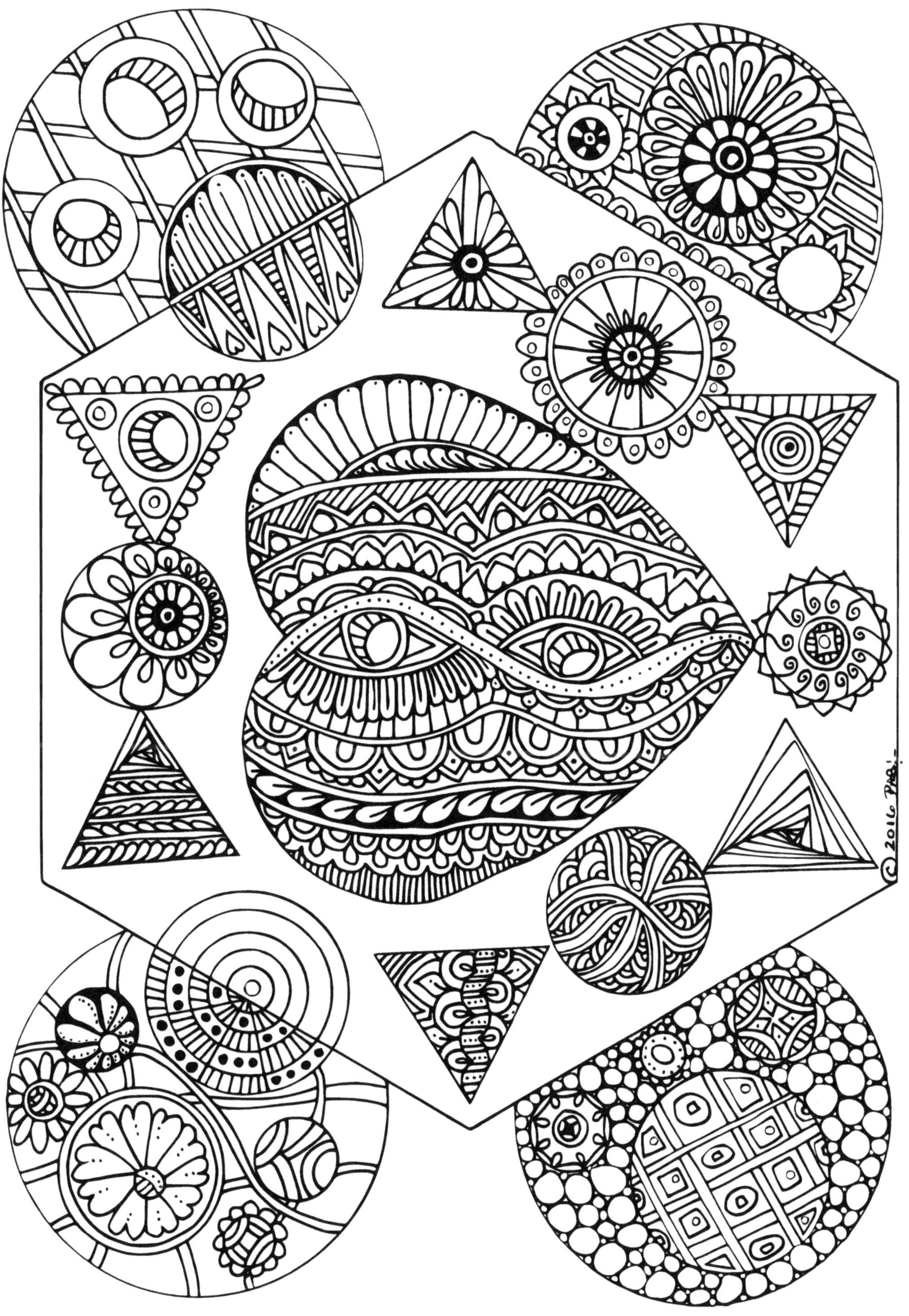

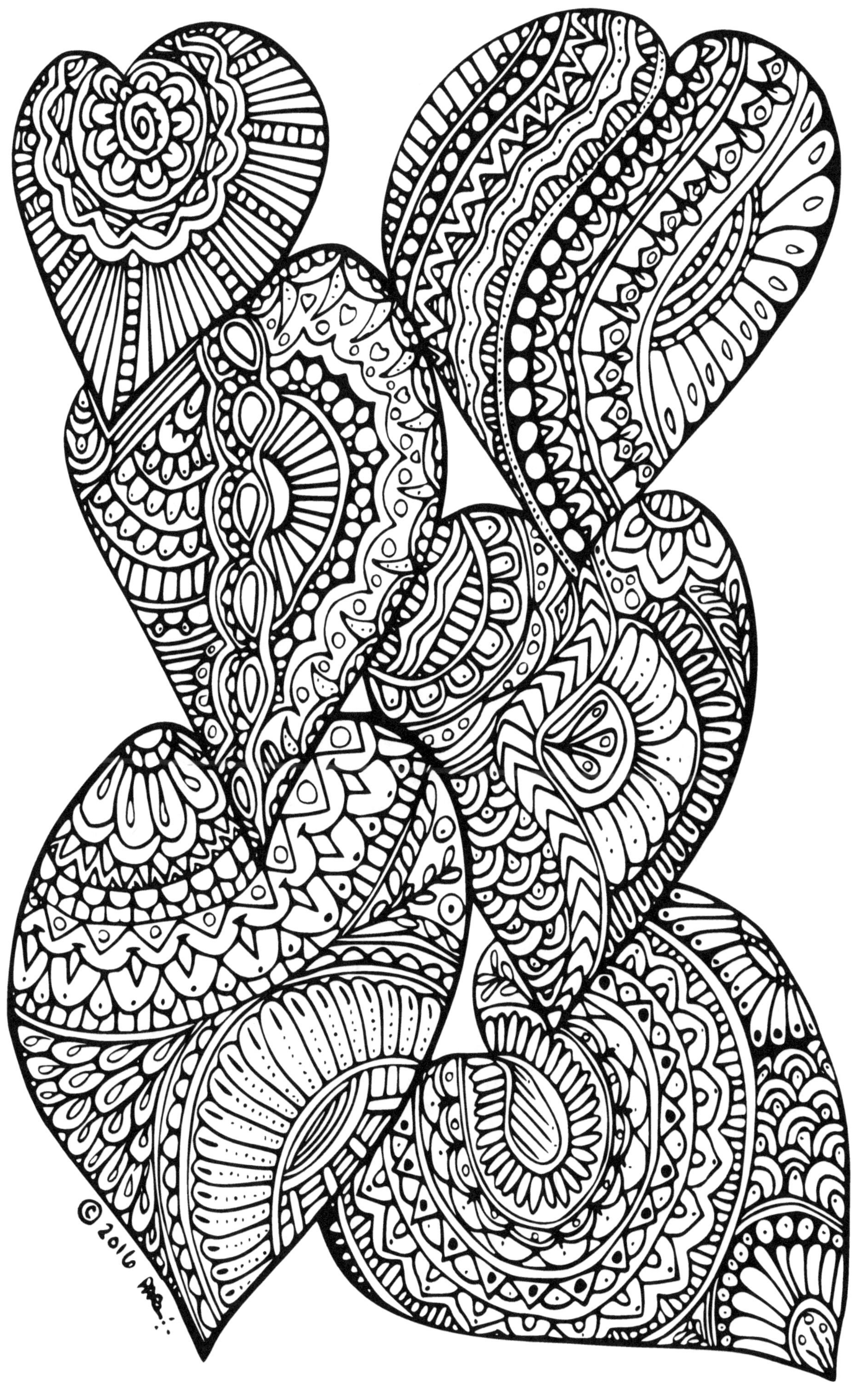
© 2016

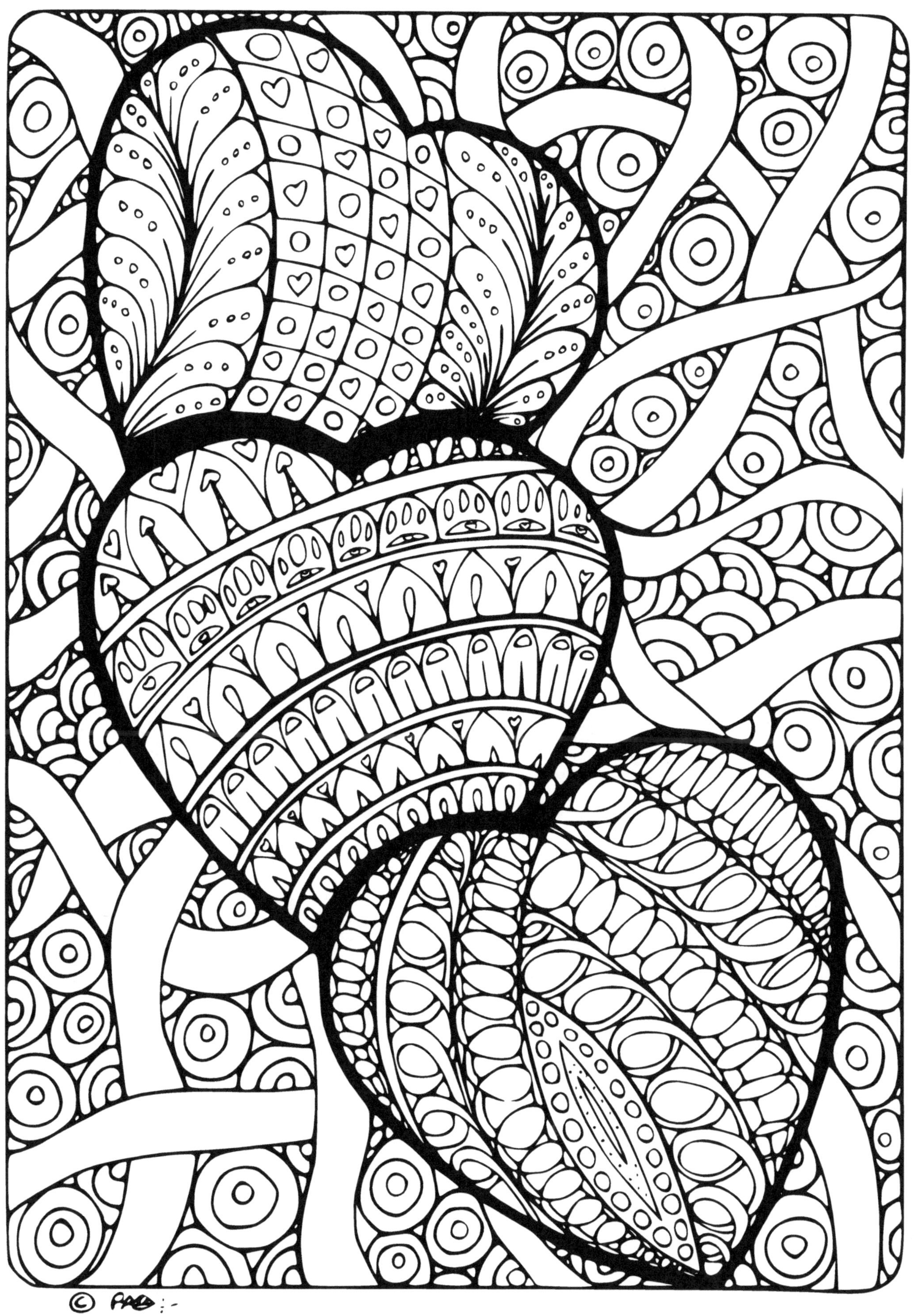

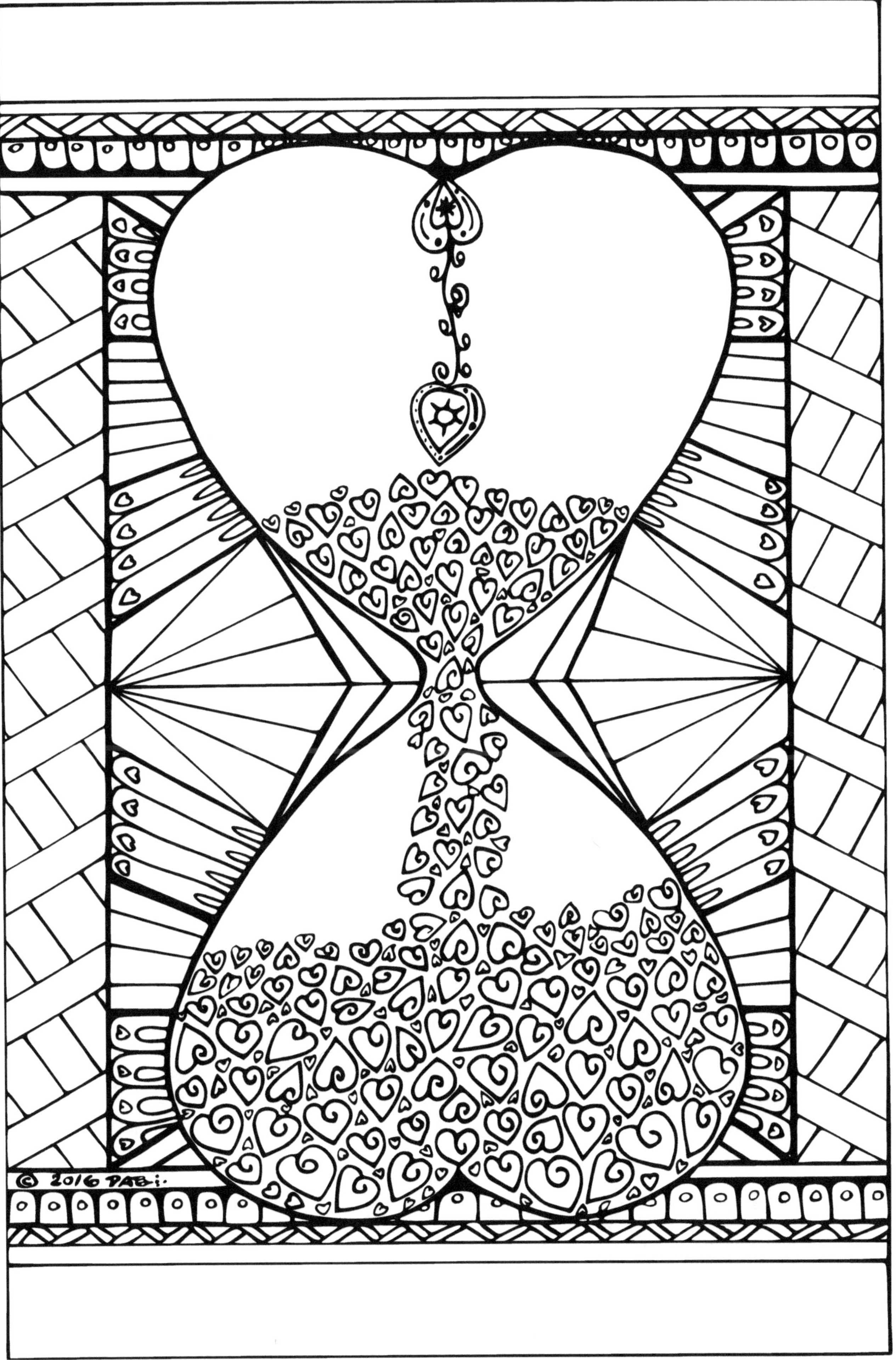
© 2016 PAB:.

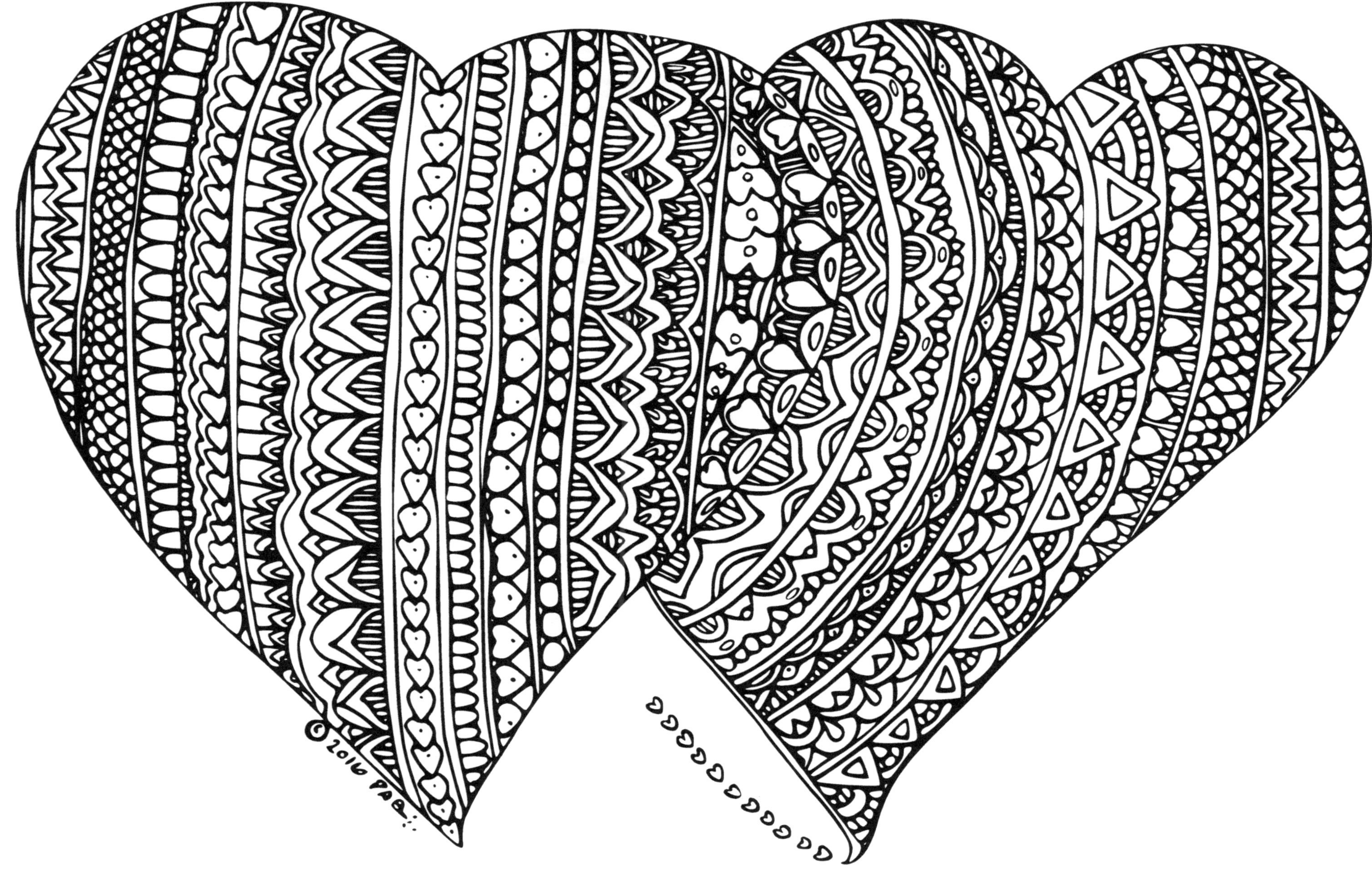
© 2016 PAB

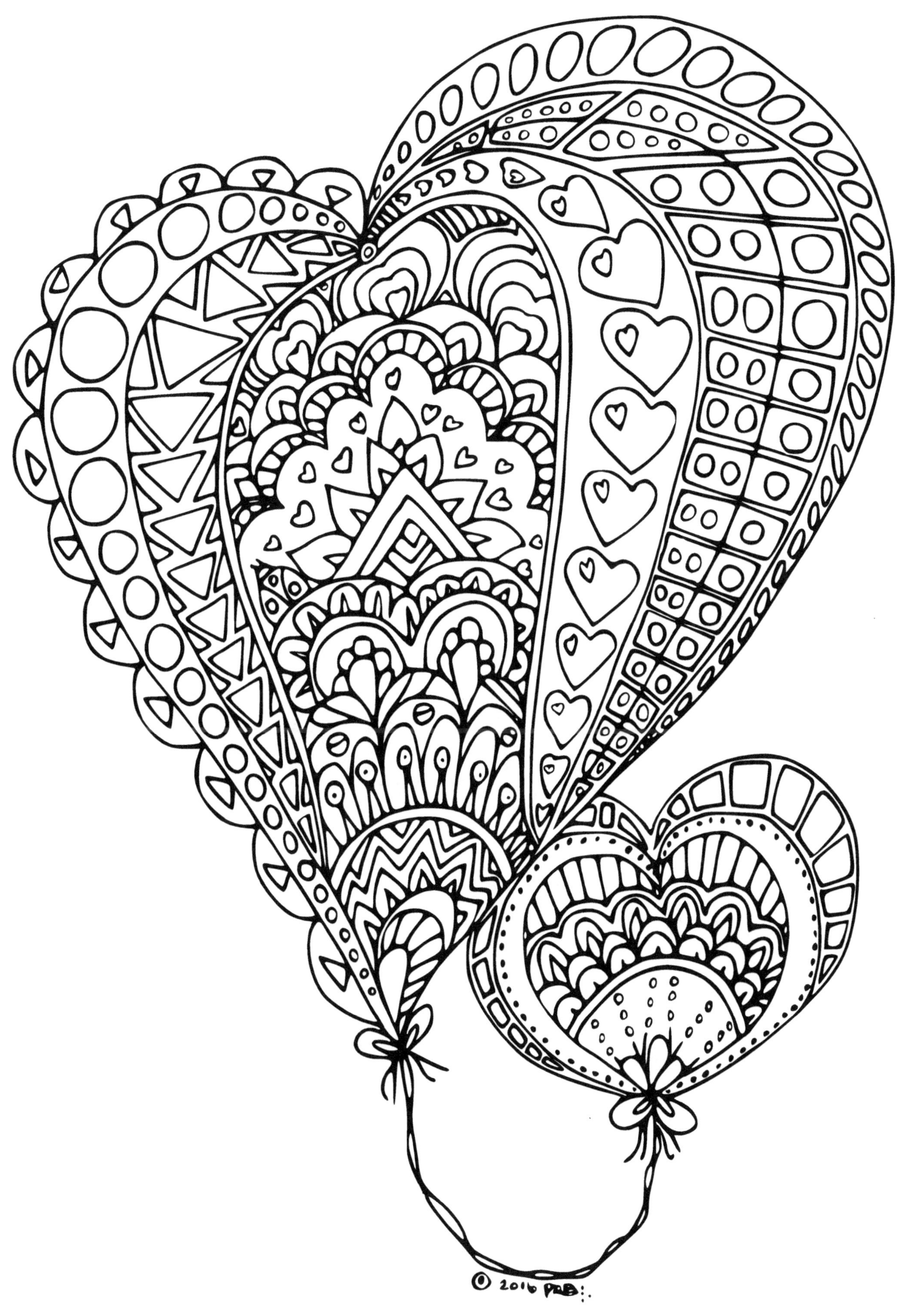

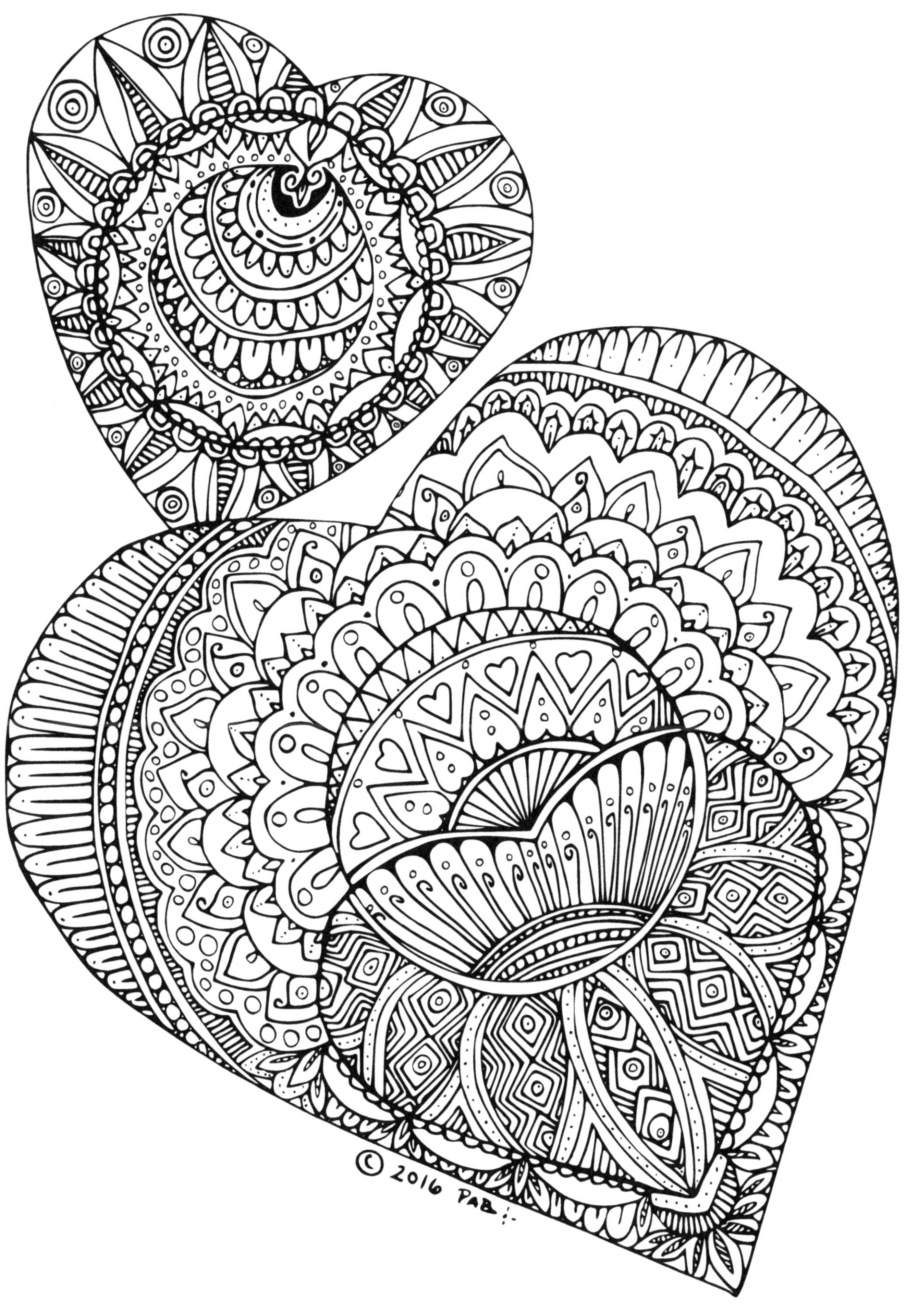
© 2016 PAB

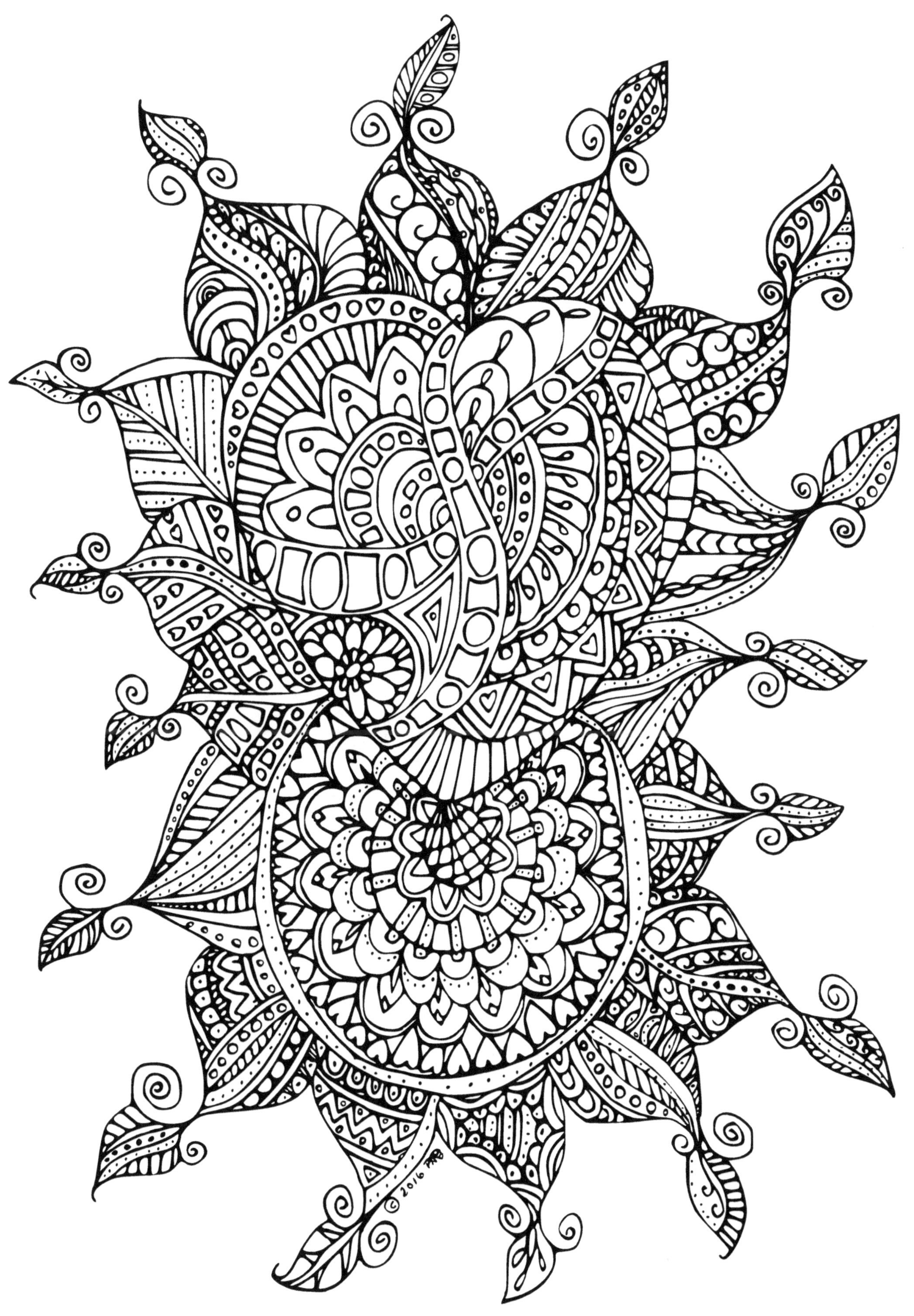
© 2016

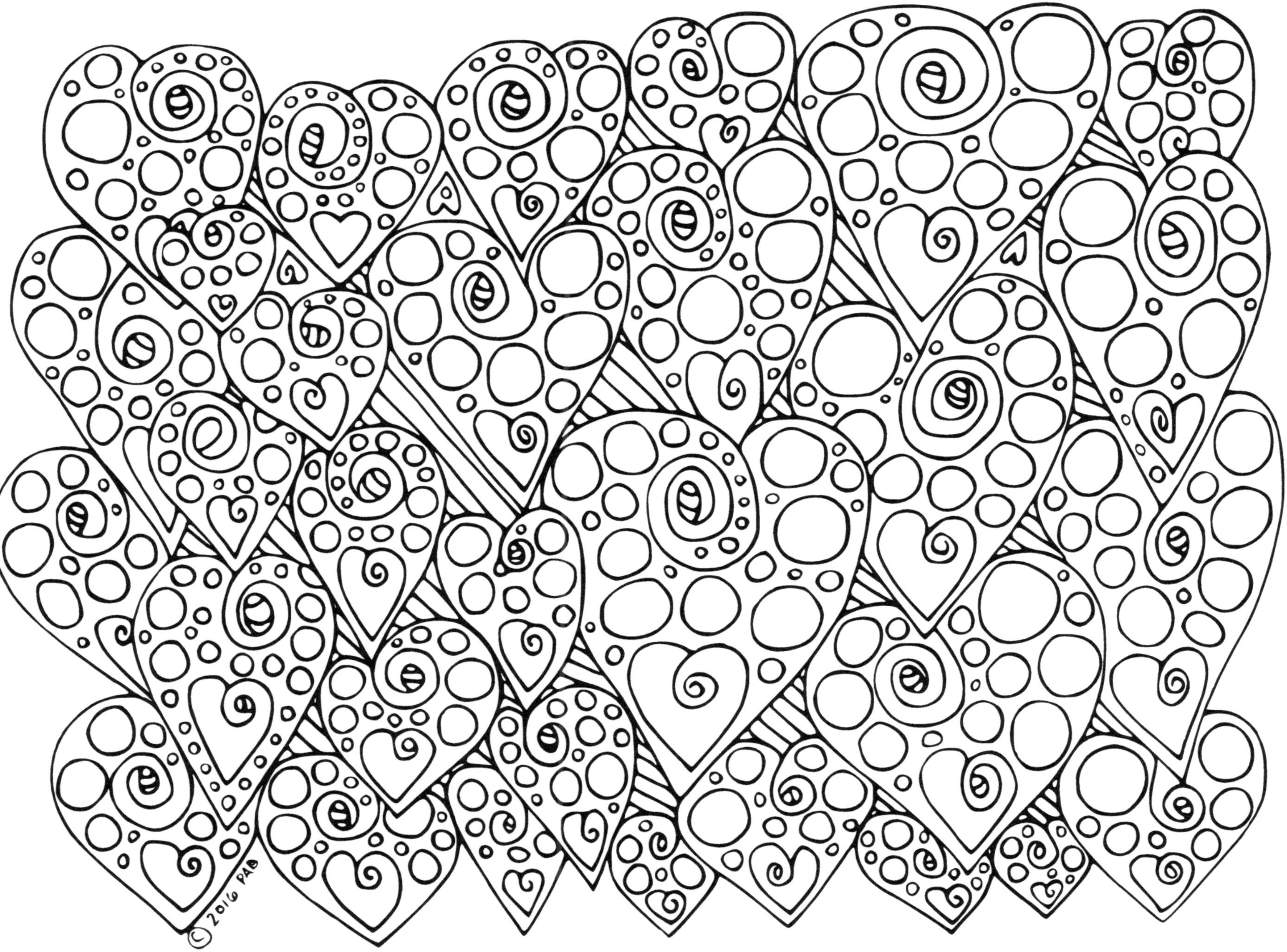
© 2016 PAB

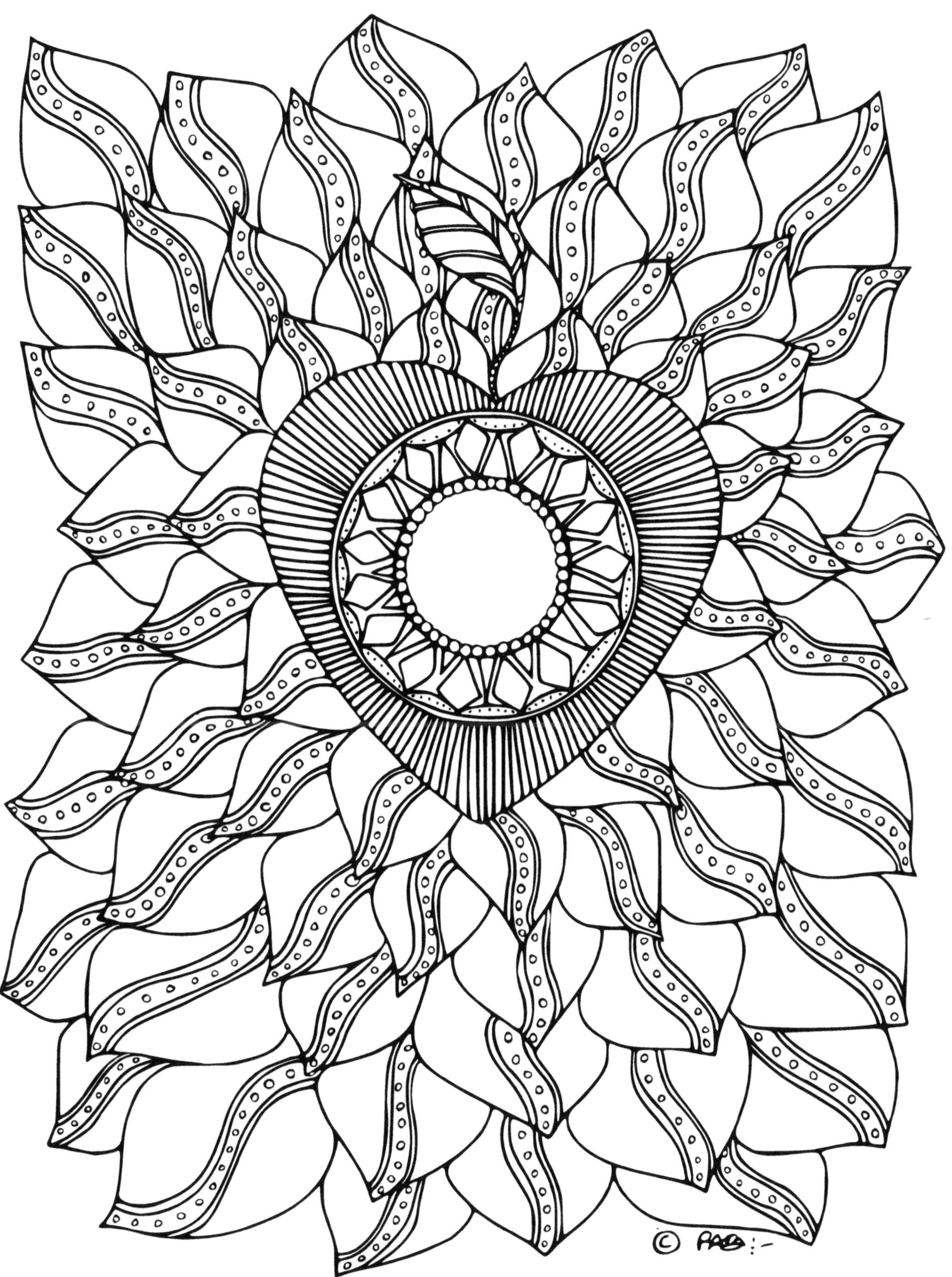

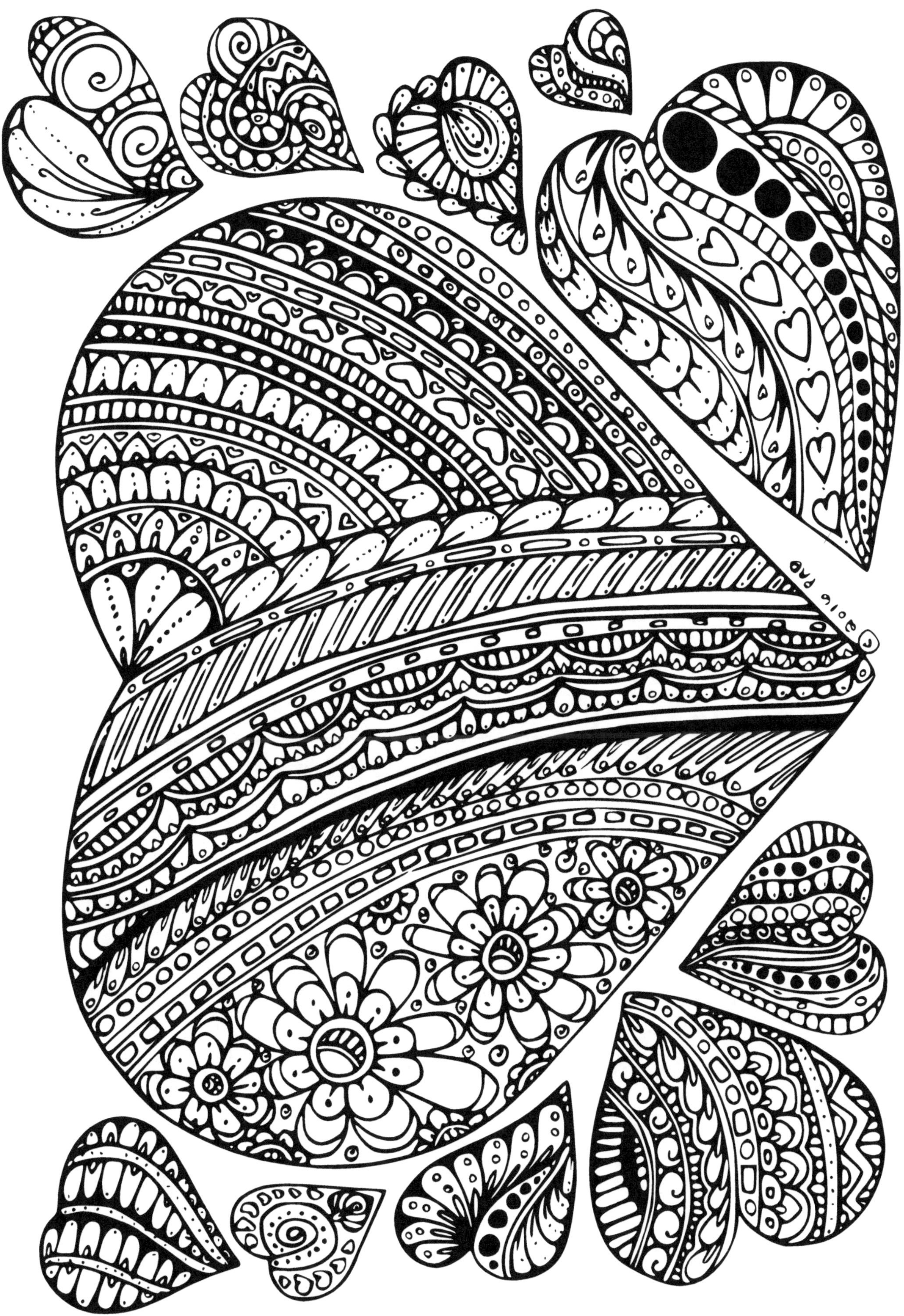

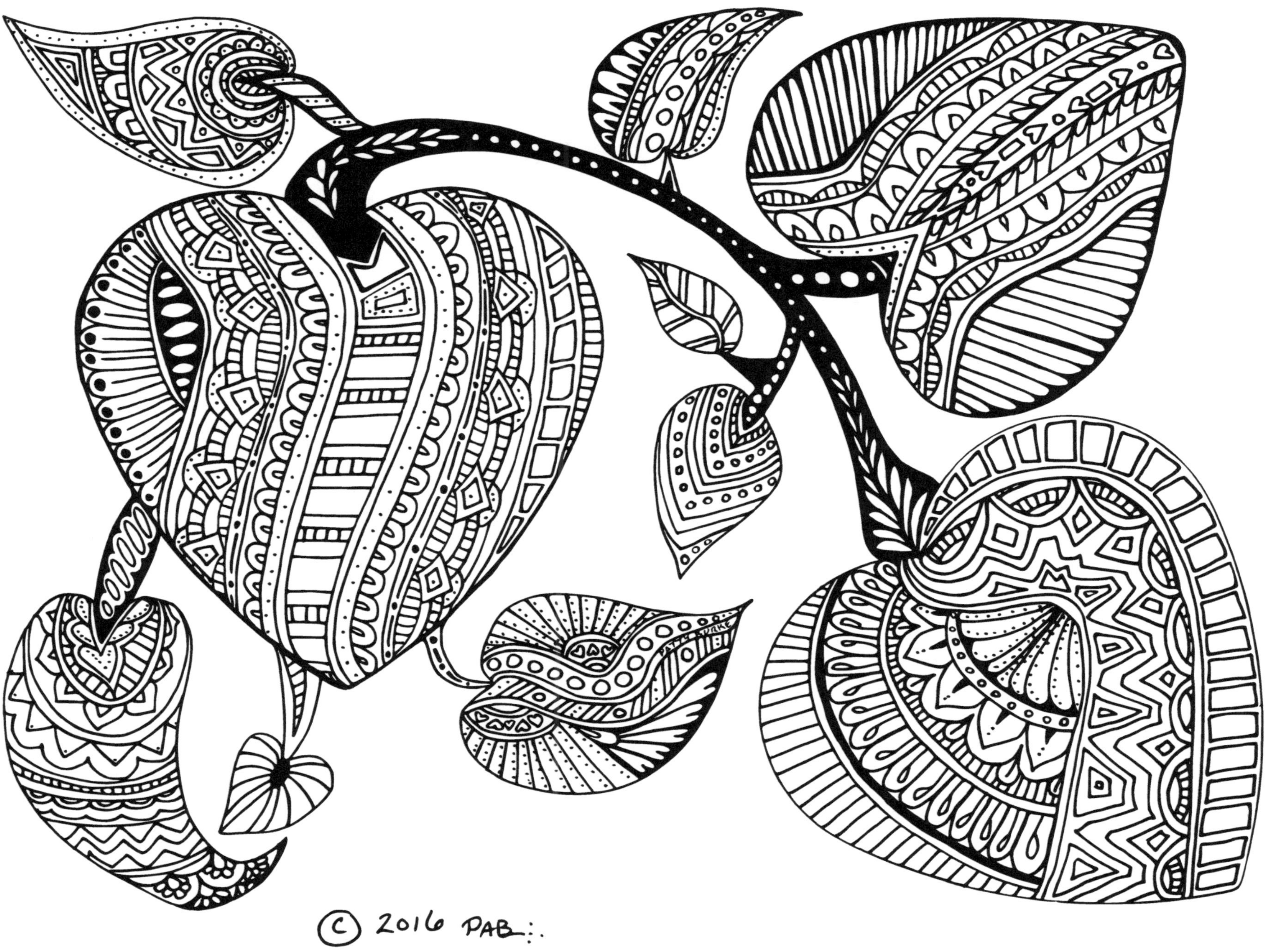
© 2016 PAB

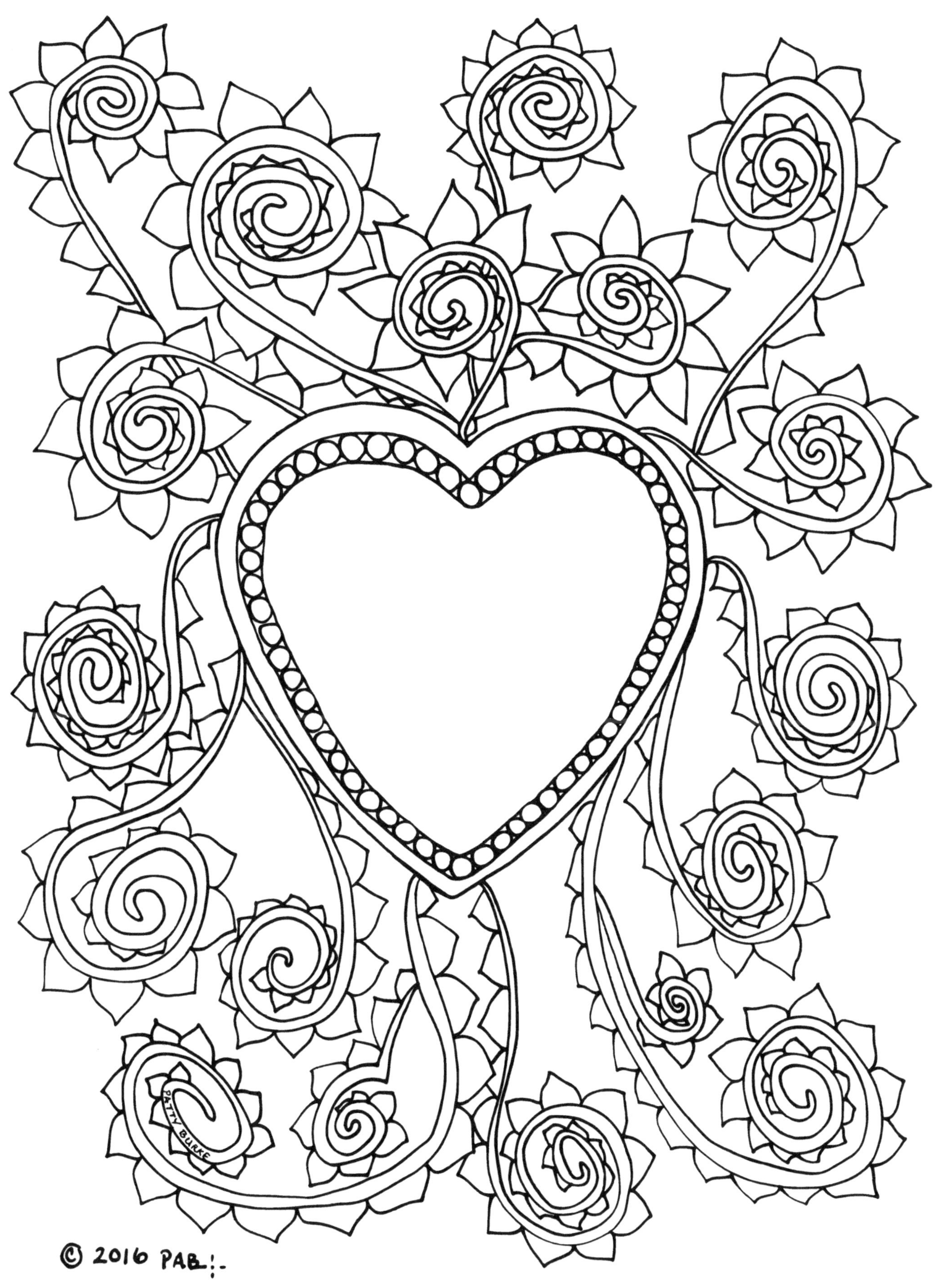
PATTY BURKE

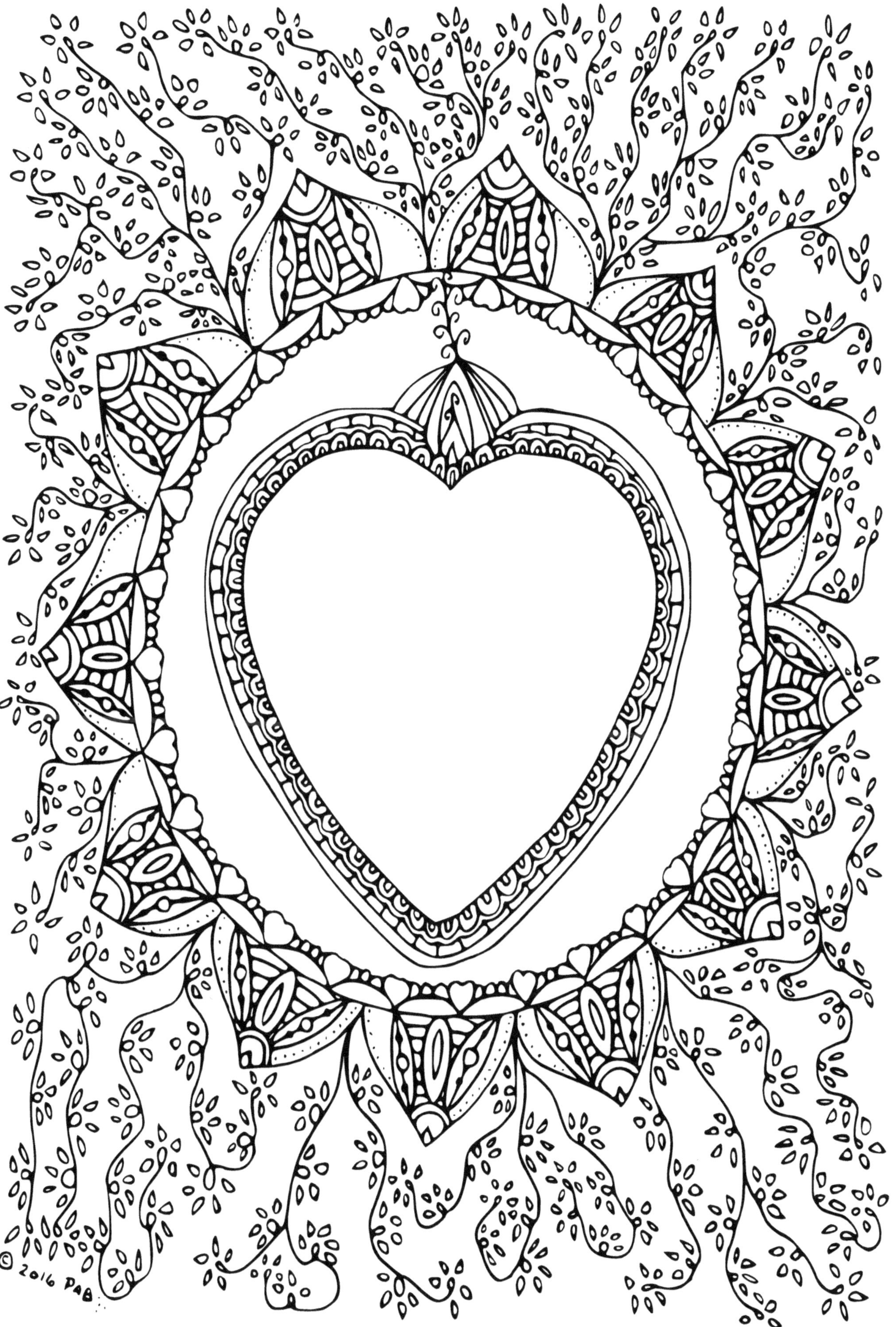
© 2016 PAB

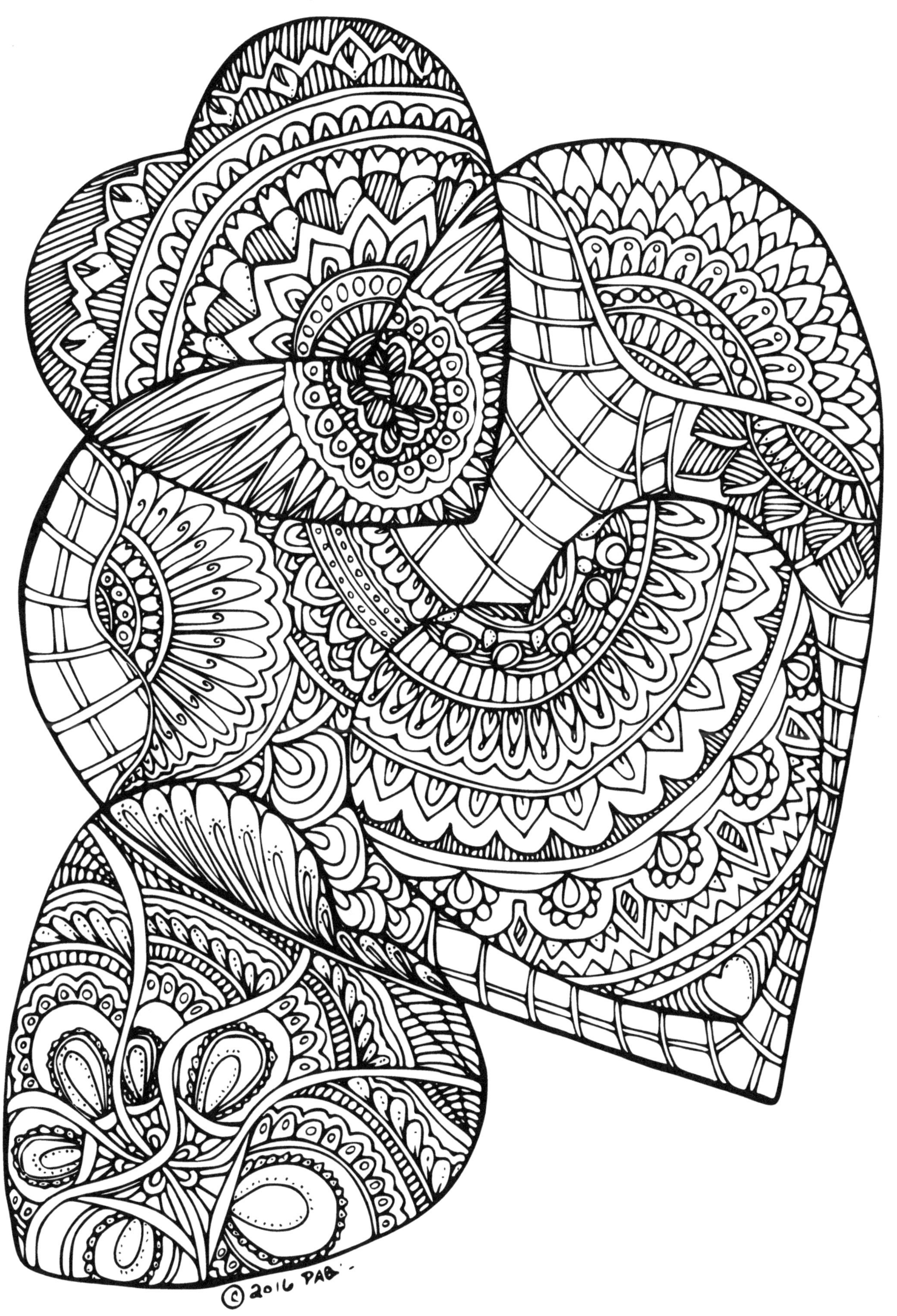

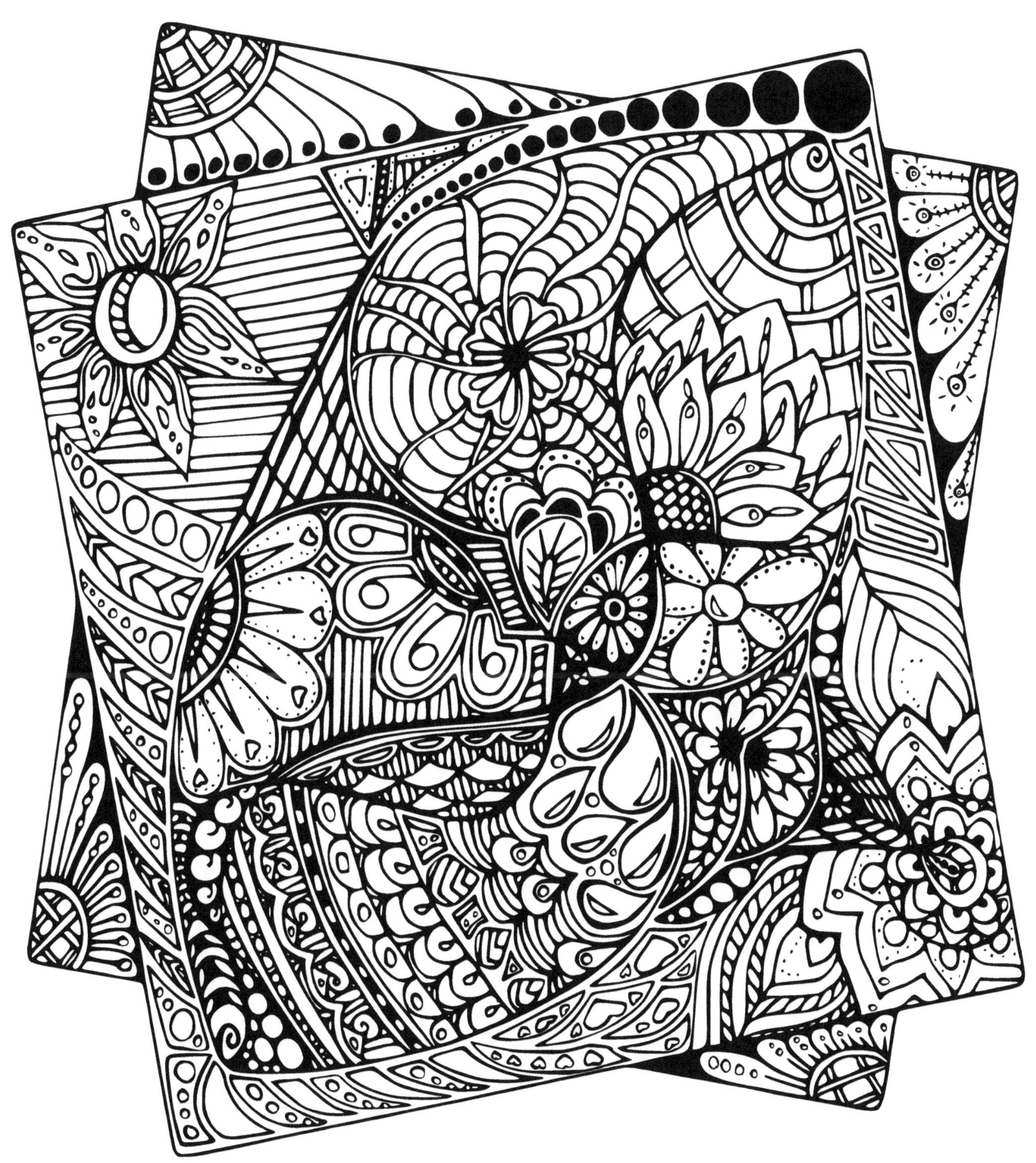

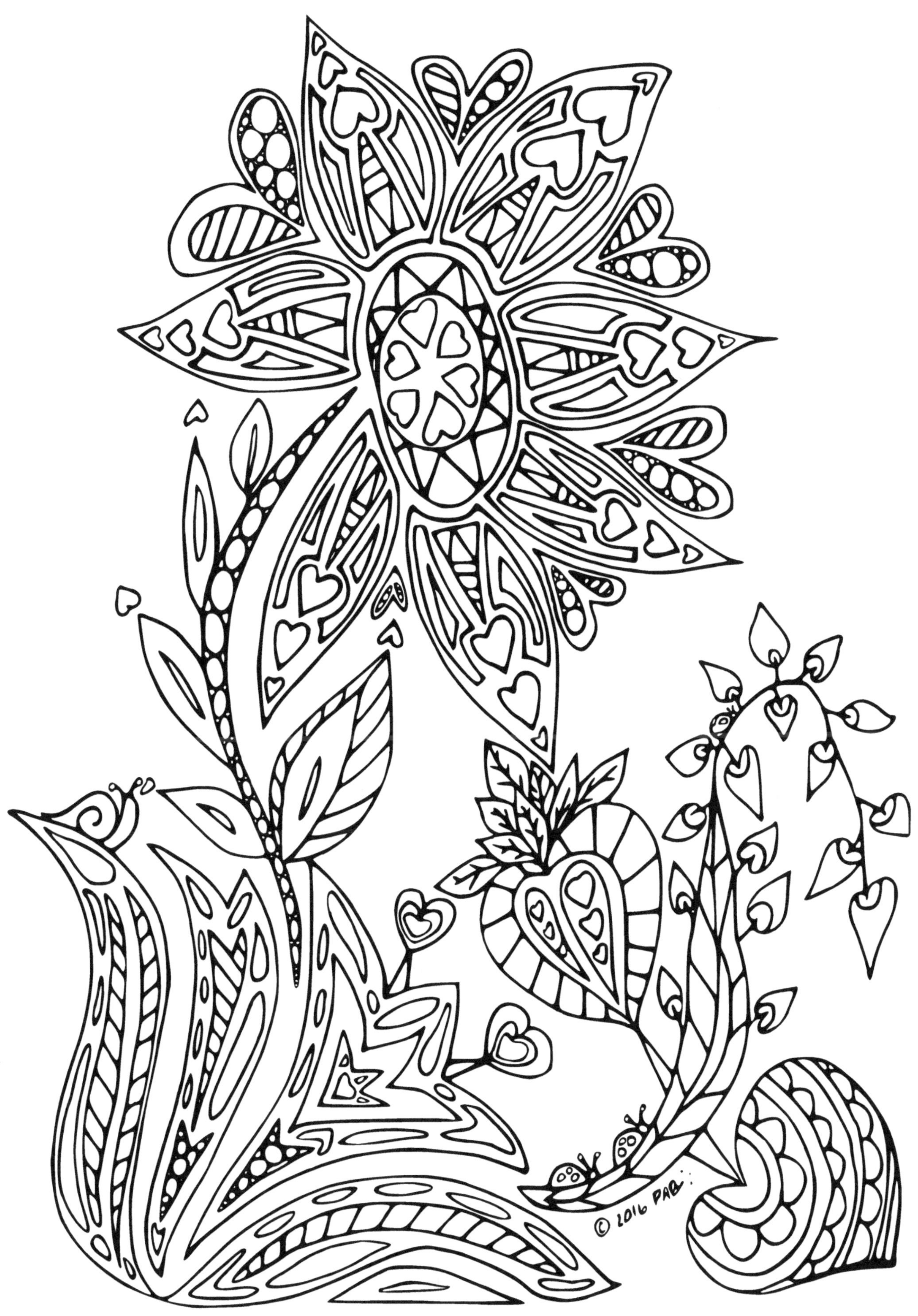
© 2016 PAB

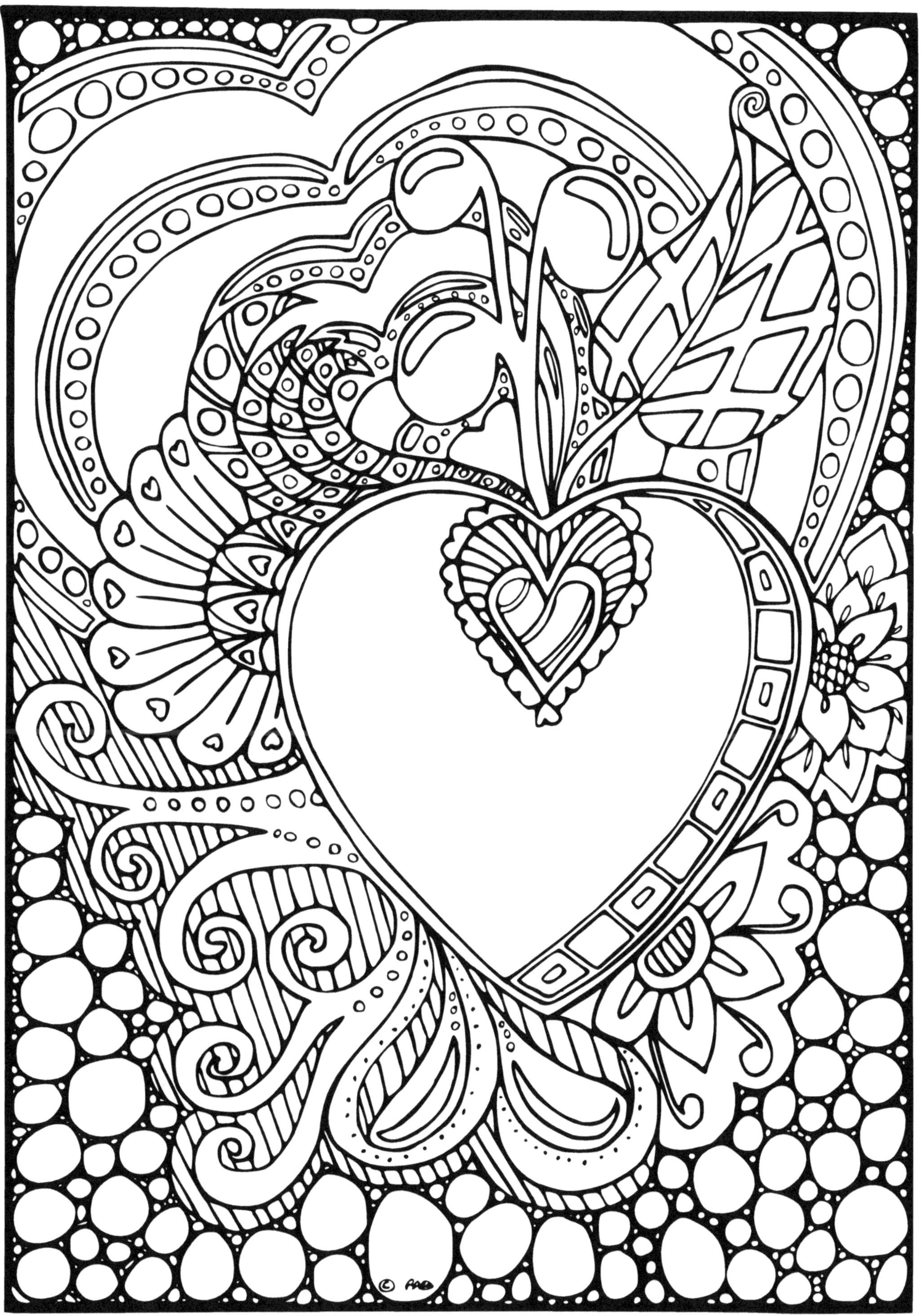

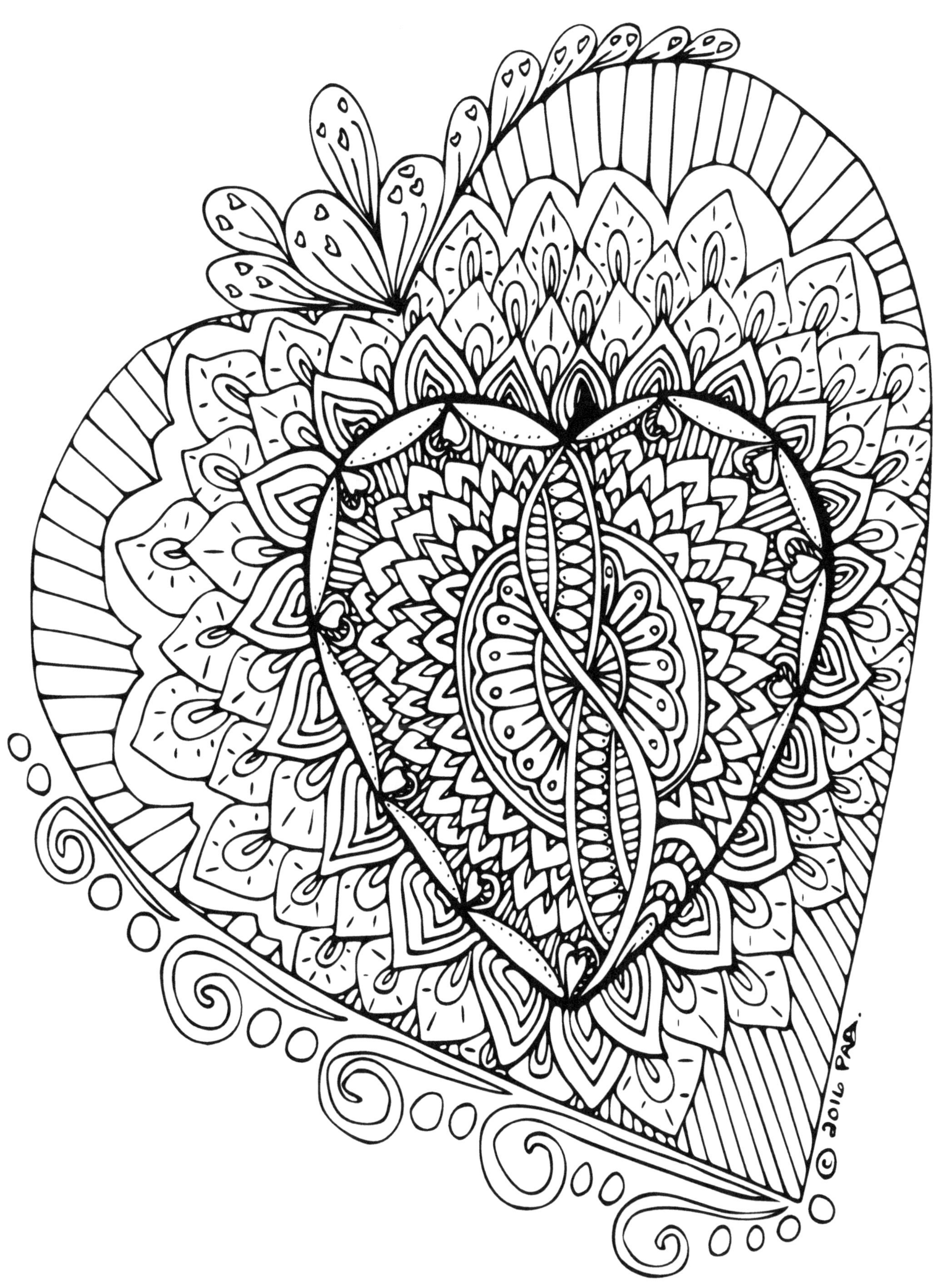
© 2016 PAA.

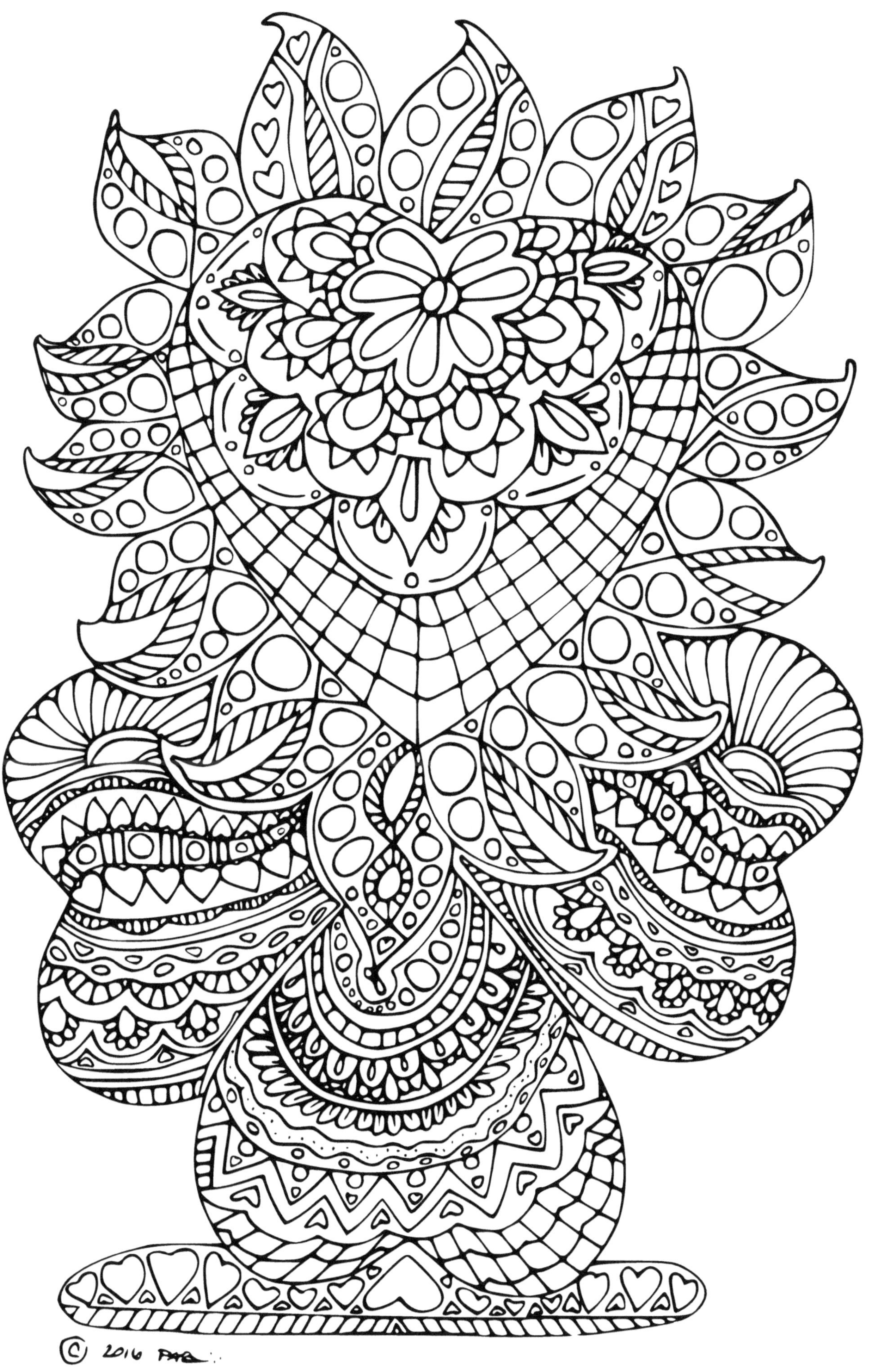
© 2016

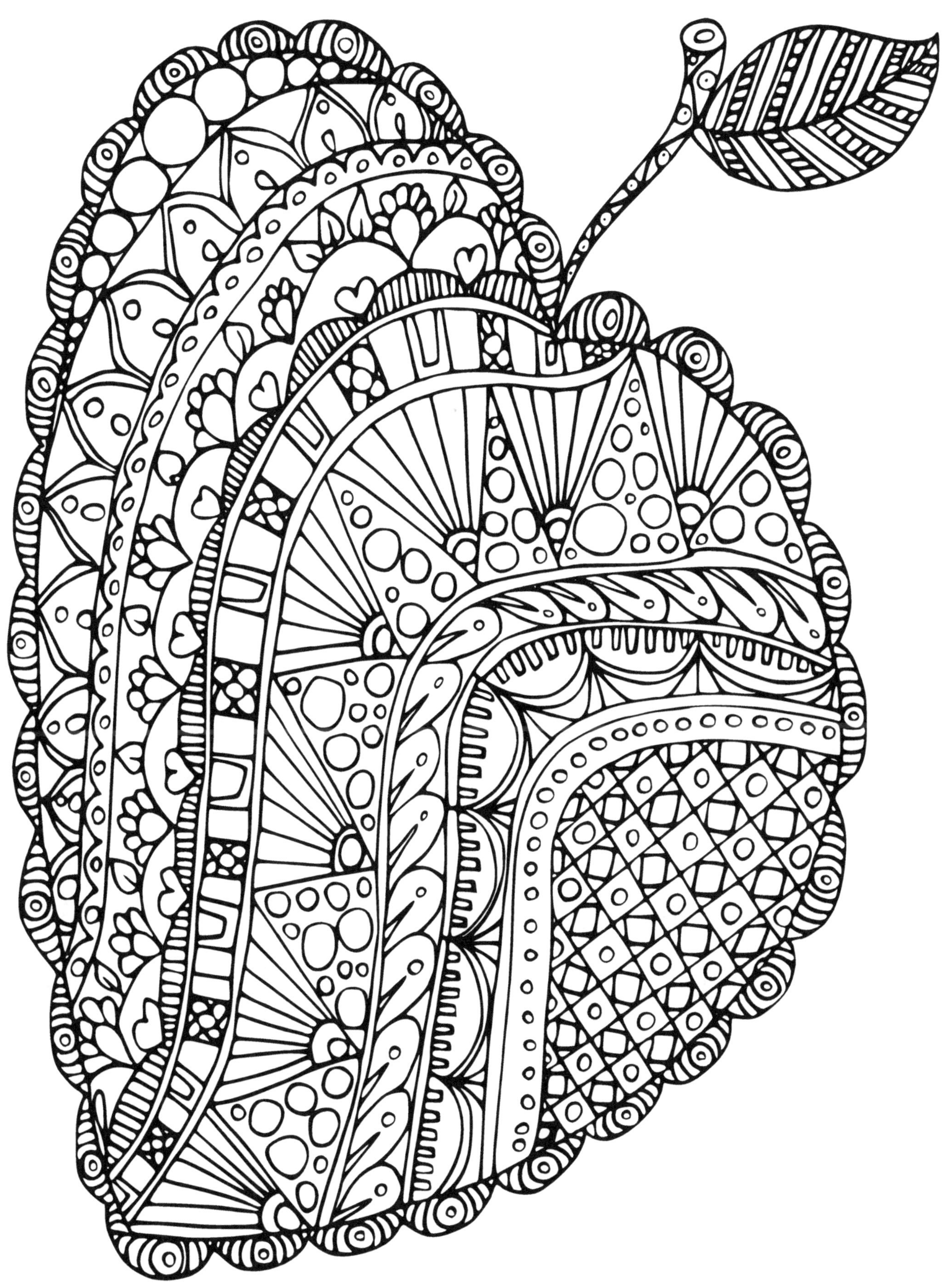

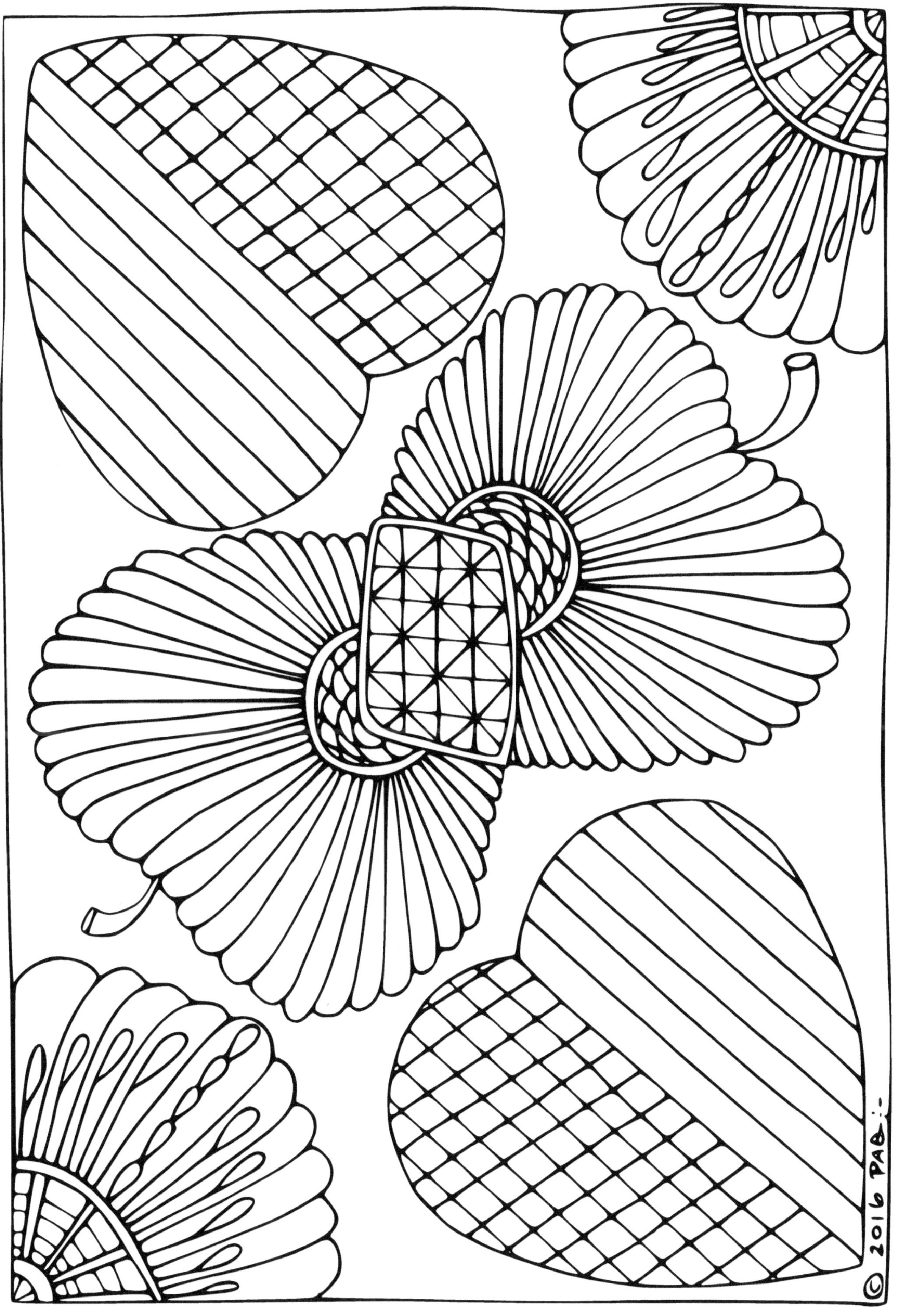
© 2016 PAB

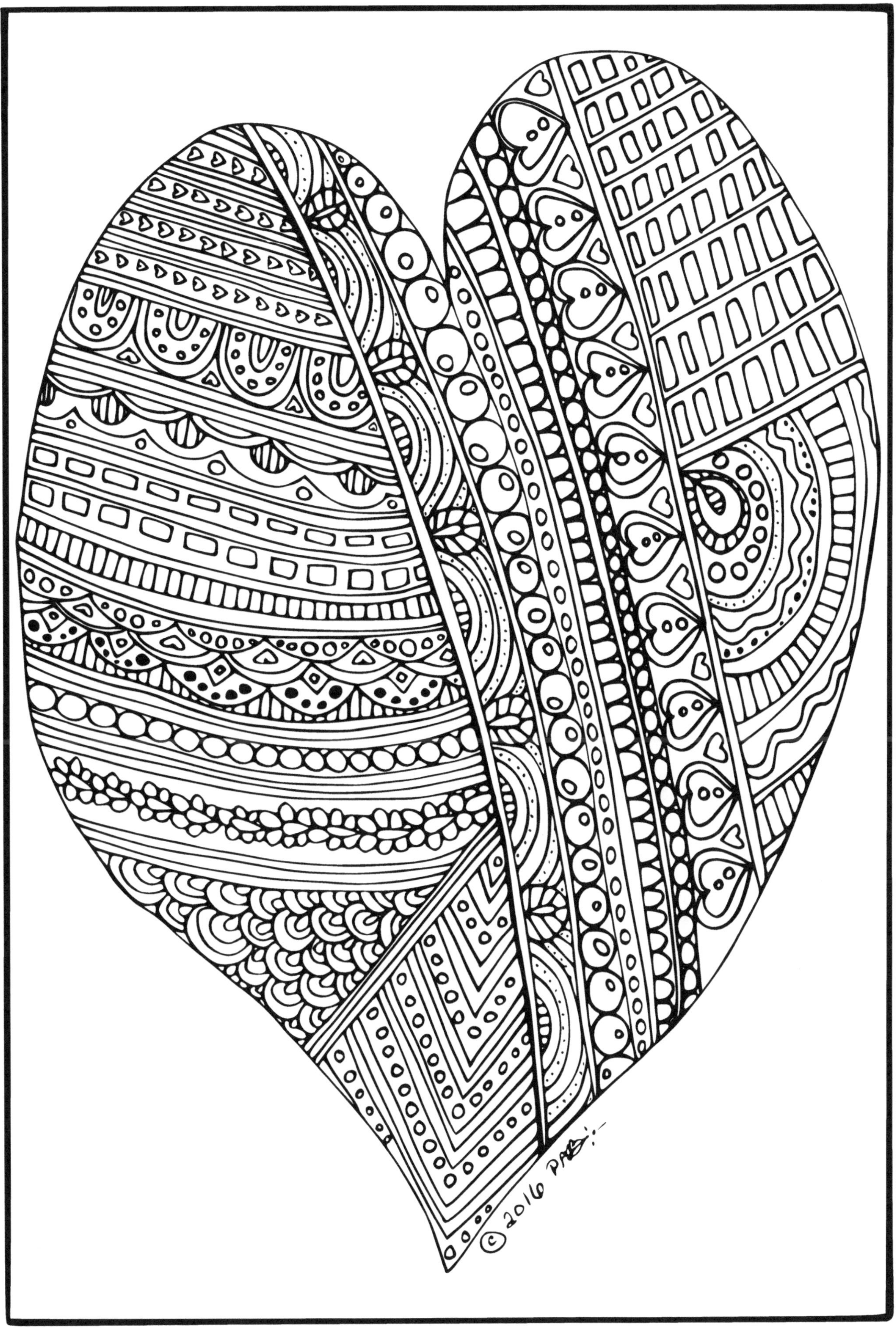
© 2016 PAB

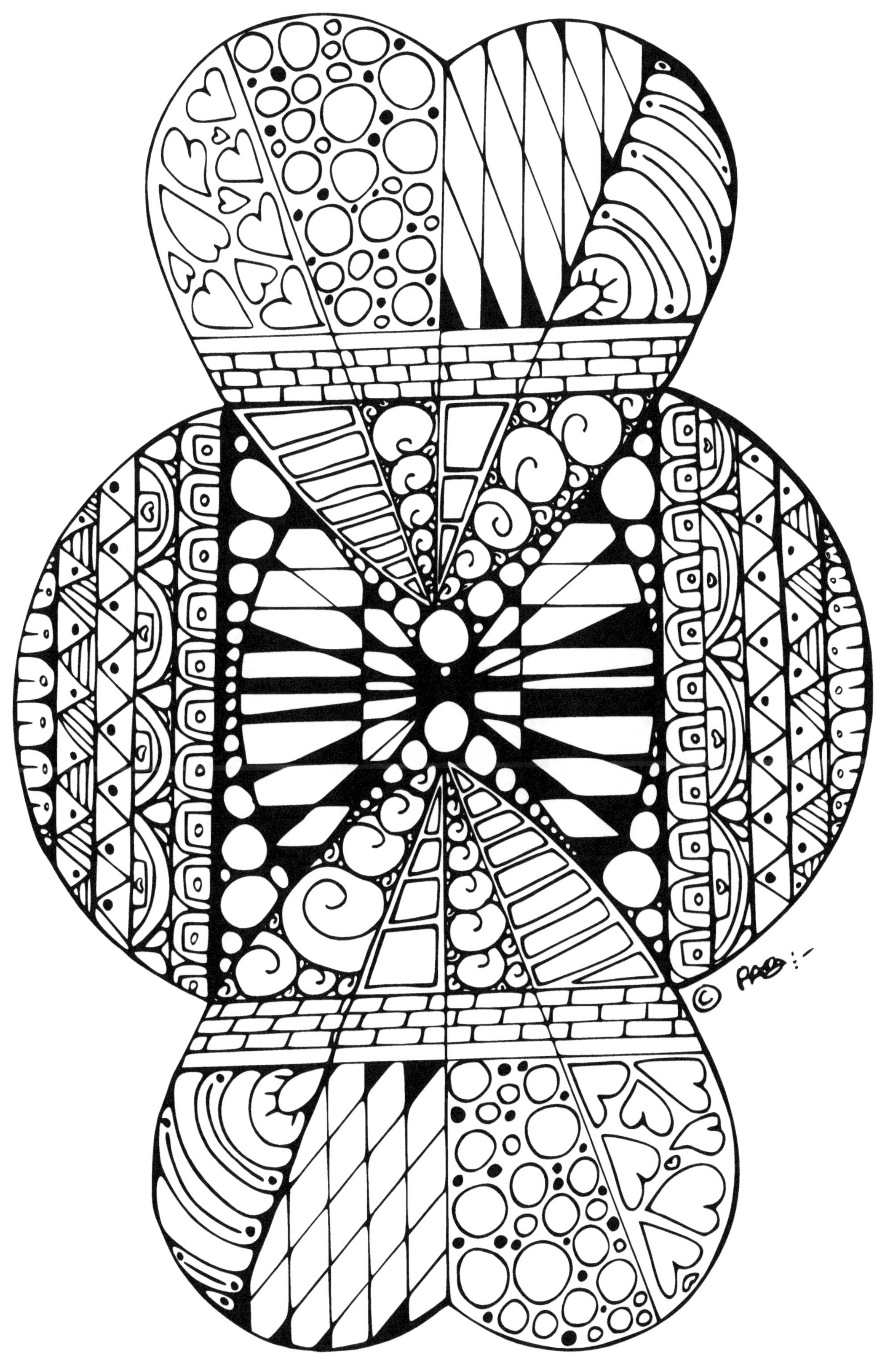

© 2016 PAB

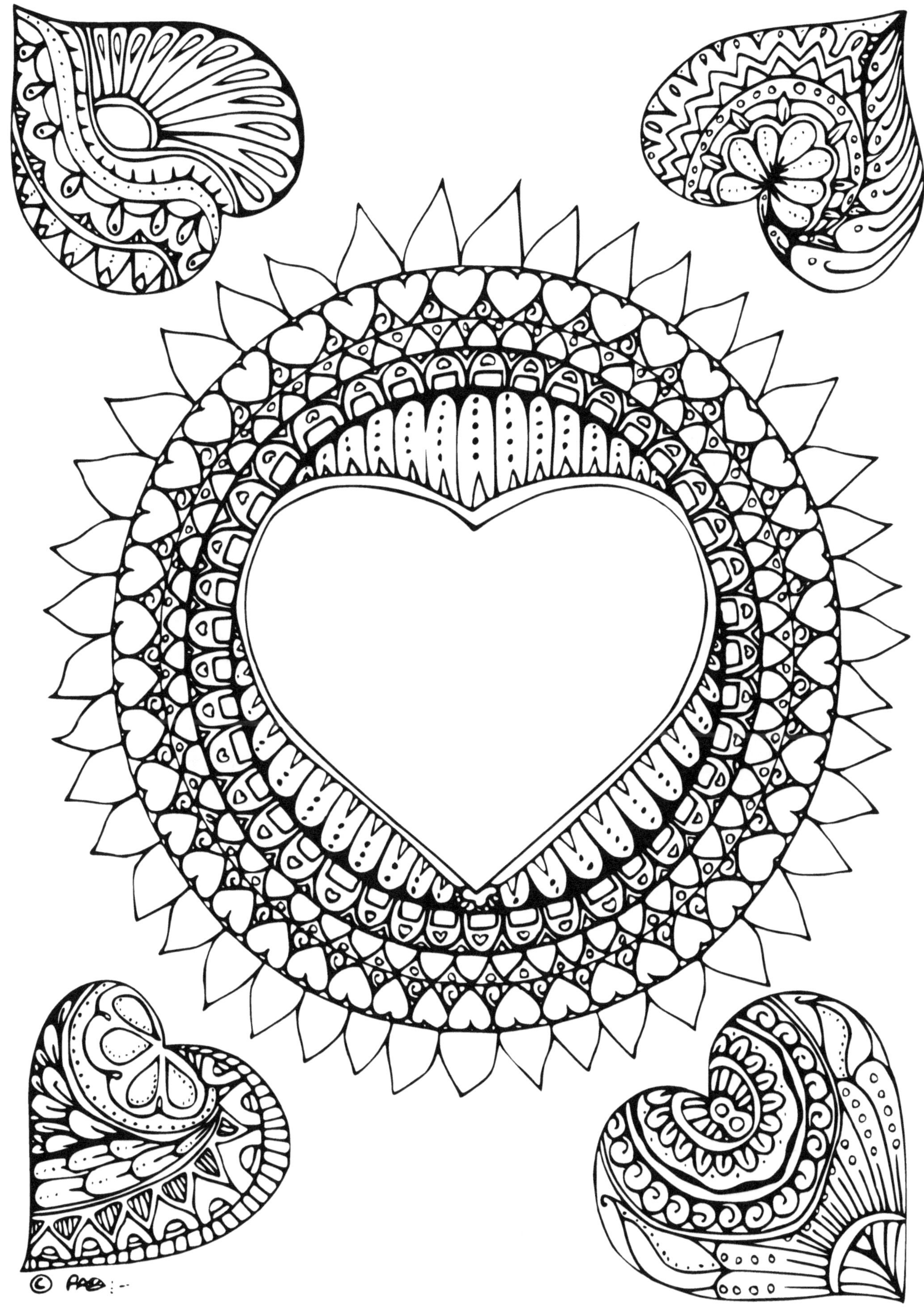

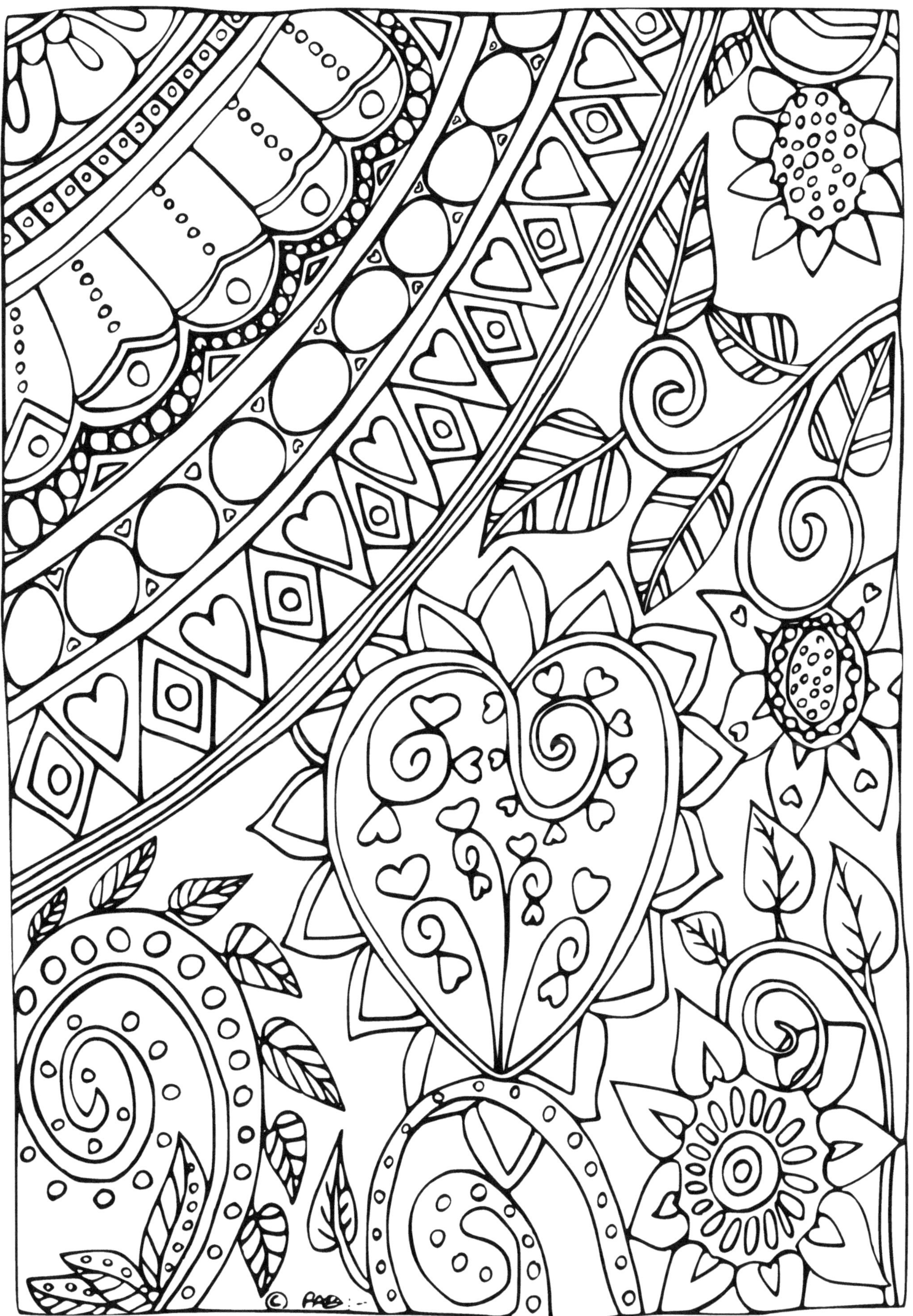

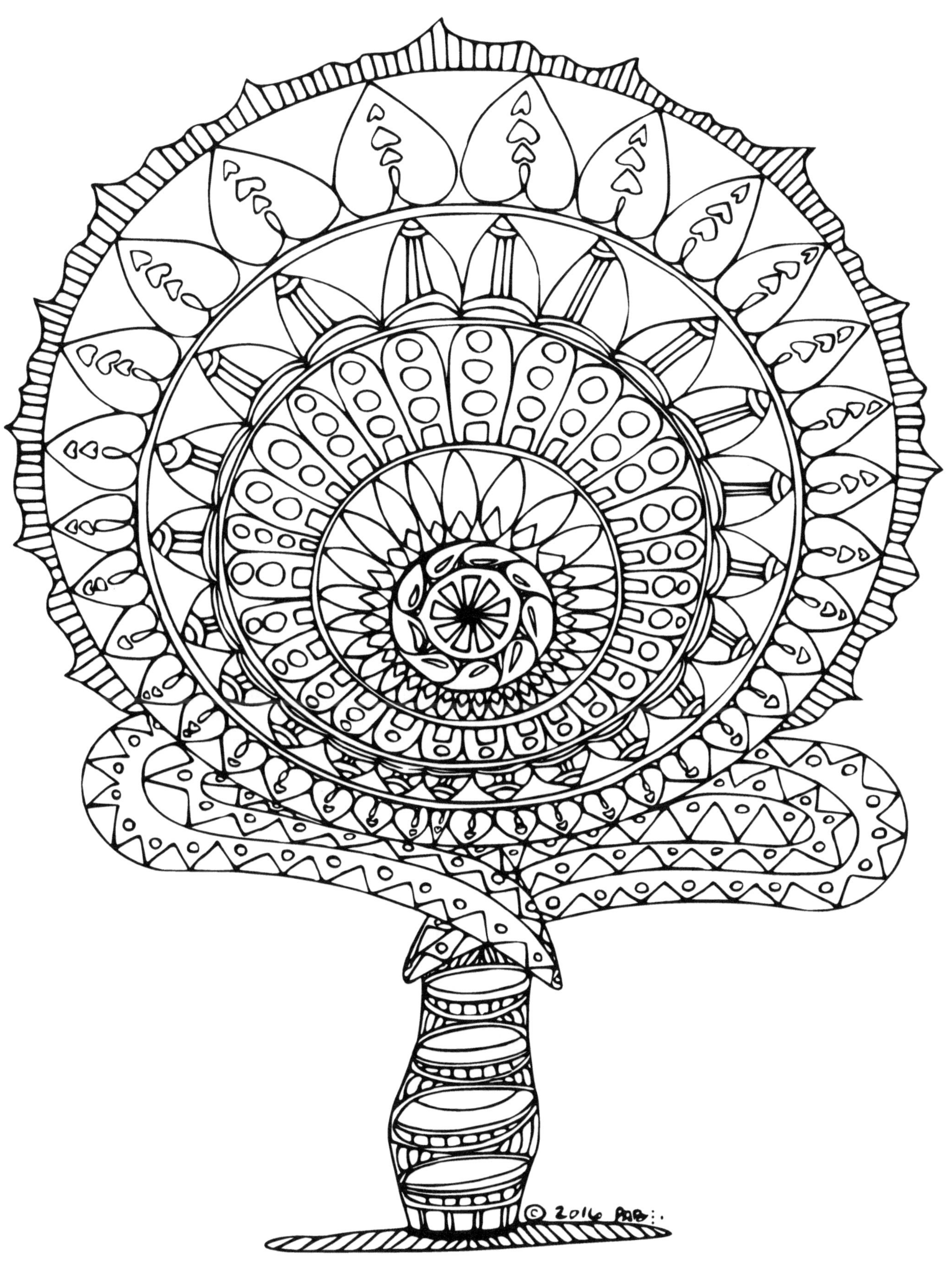
© 2016 PAB

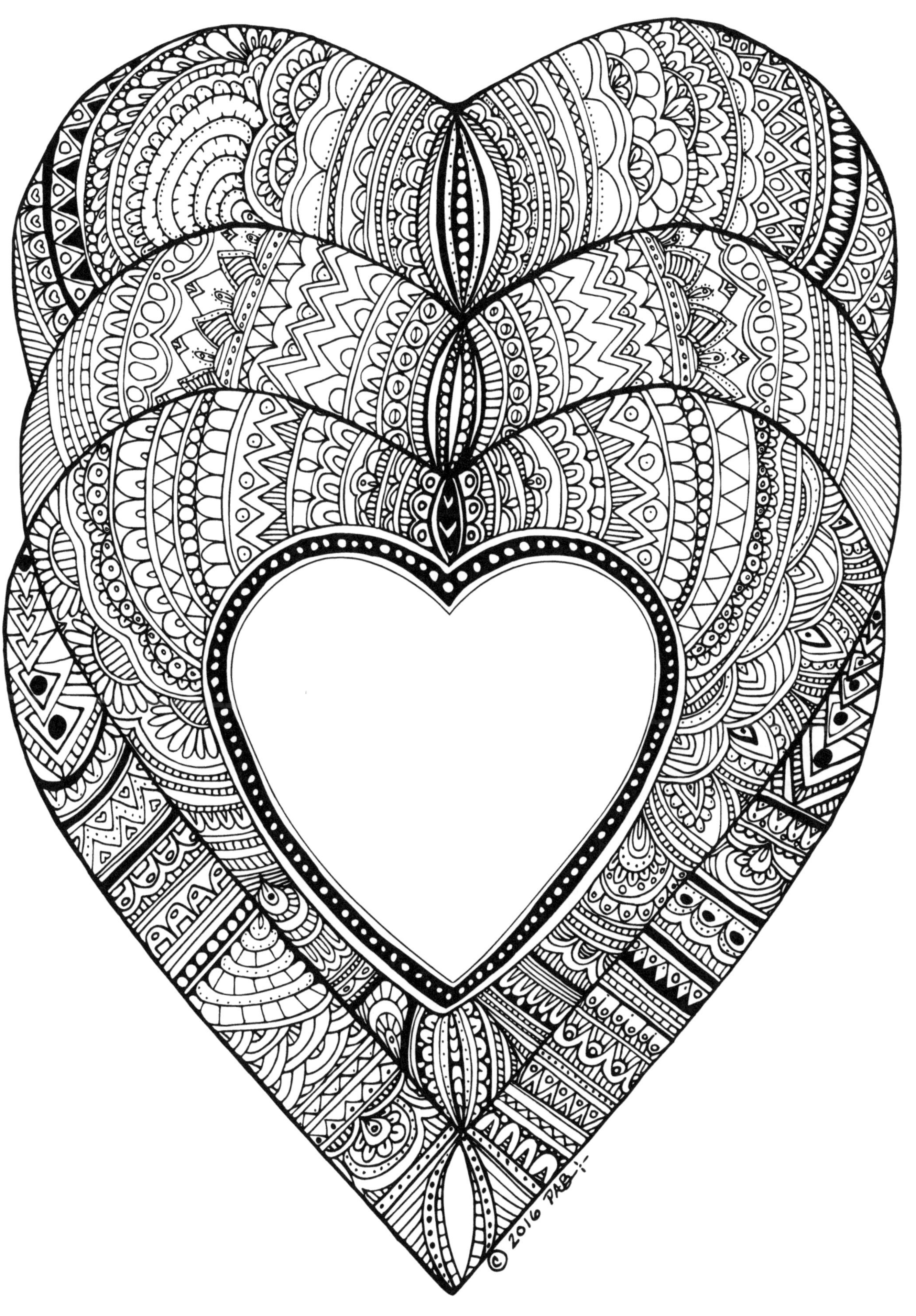
© 2016 PAB

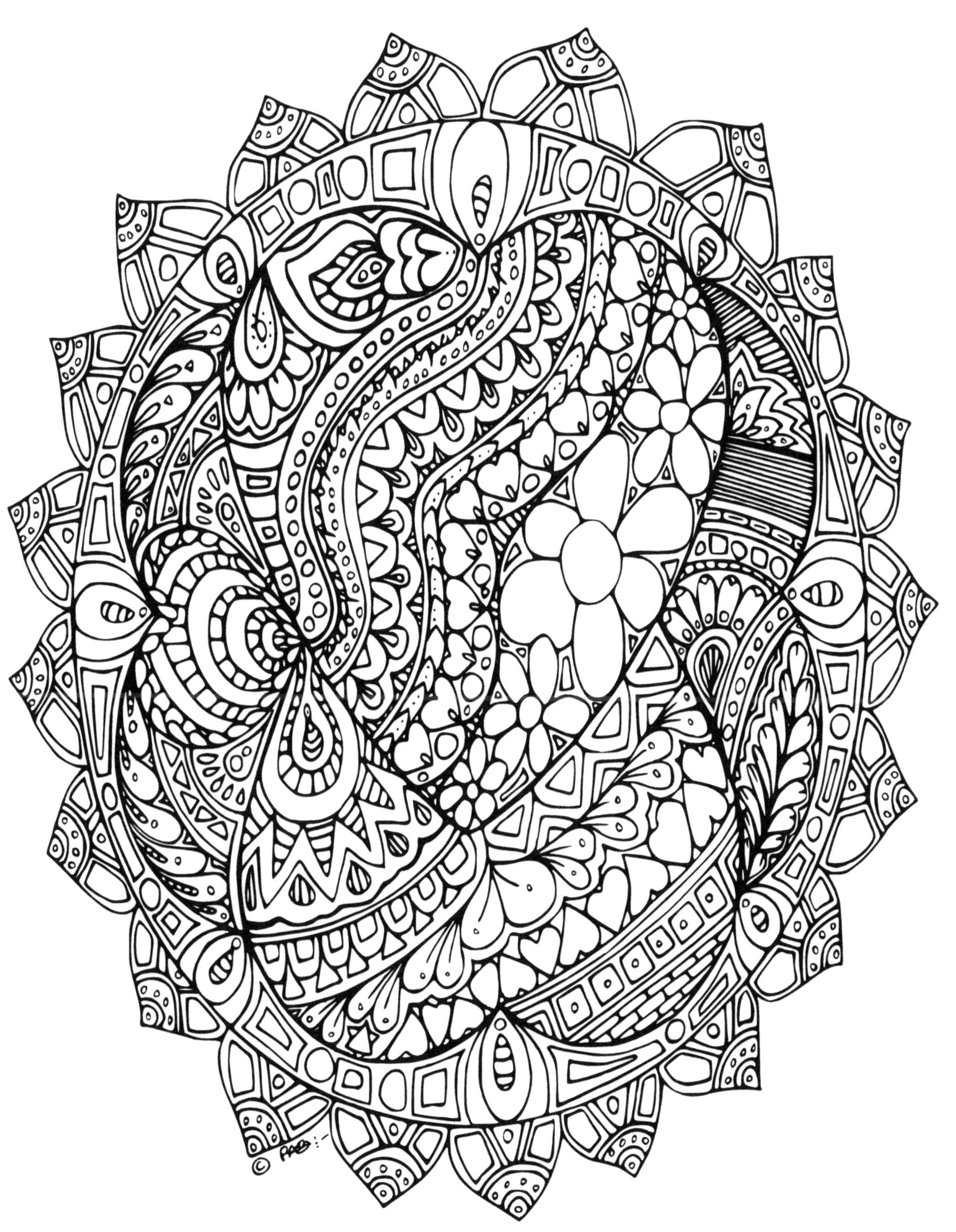

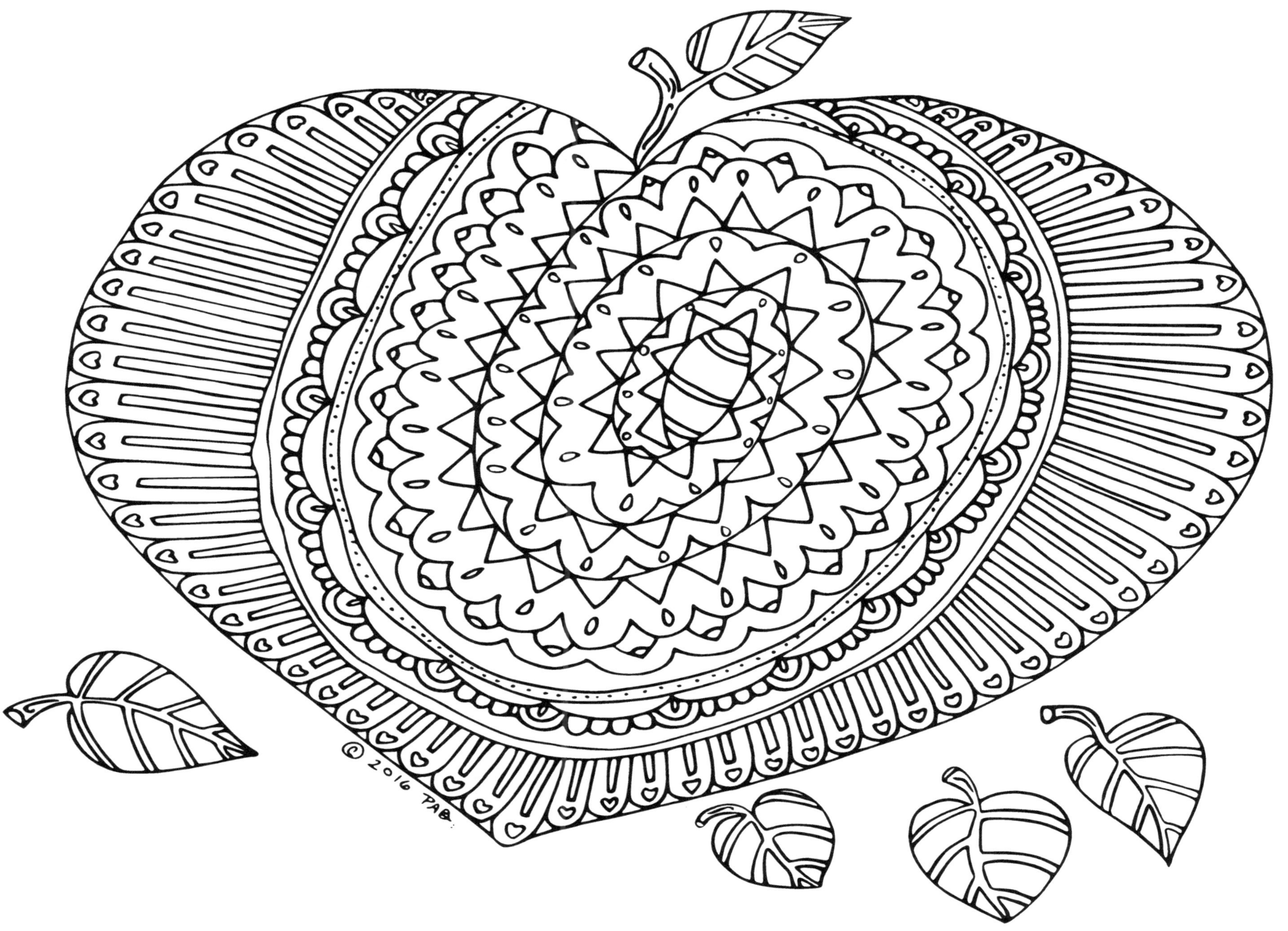
© 2016 PAB.

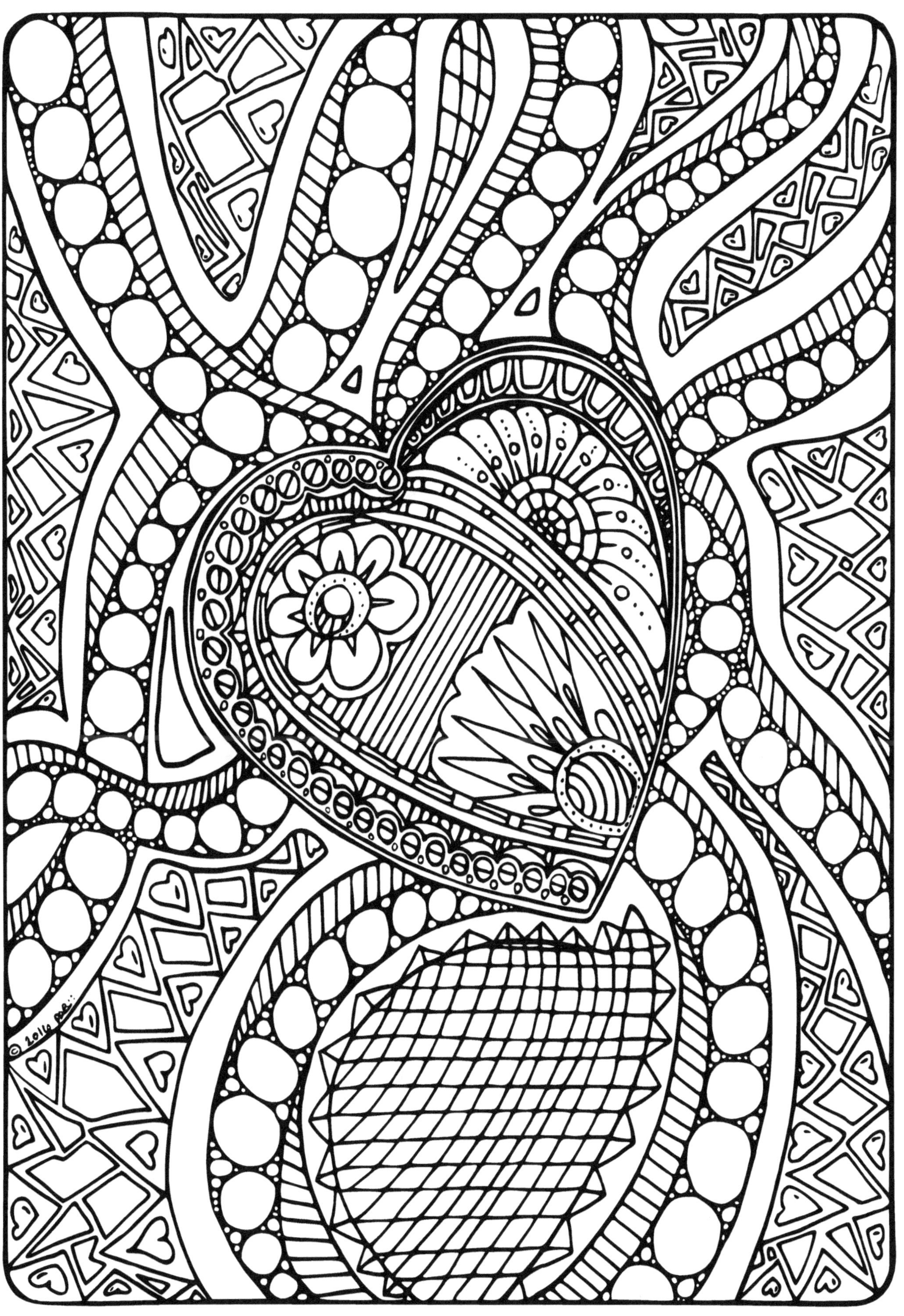
© 2016

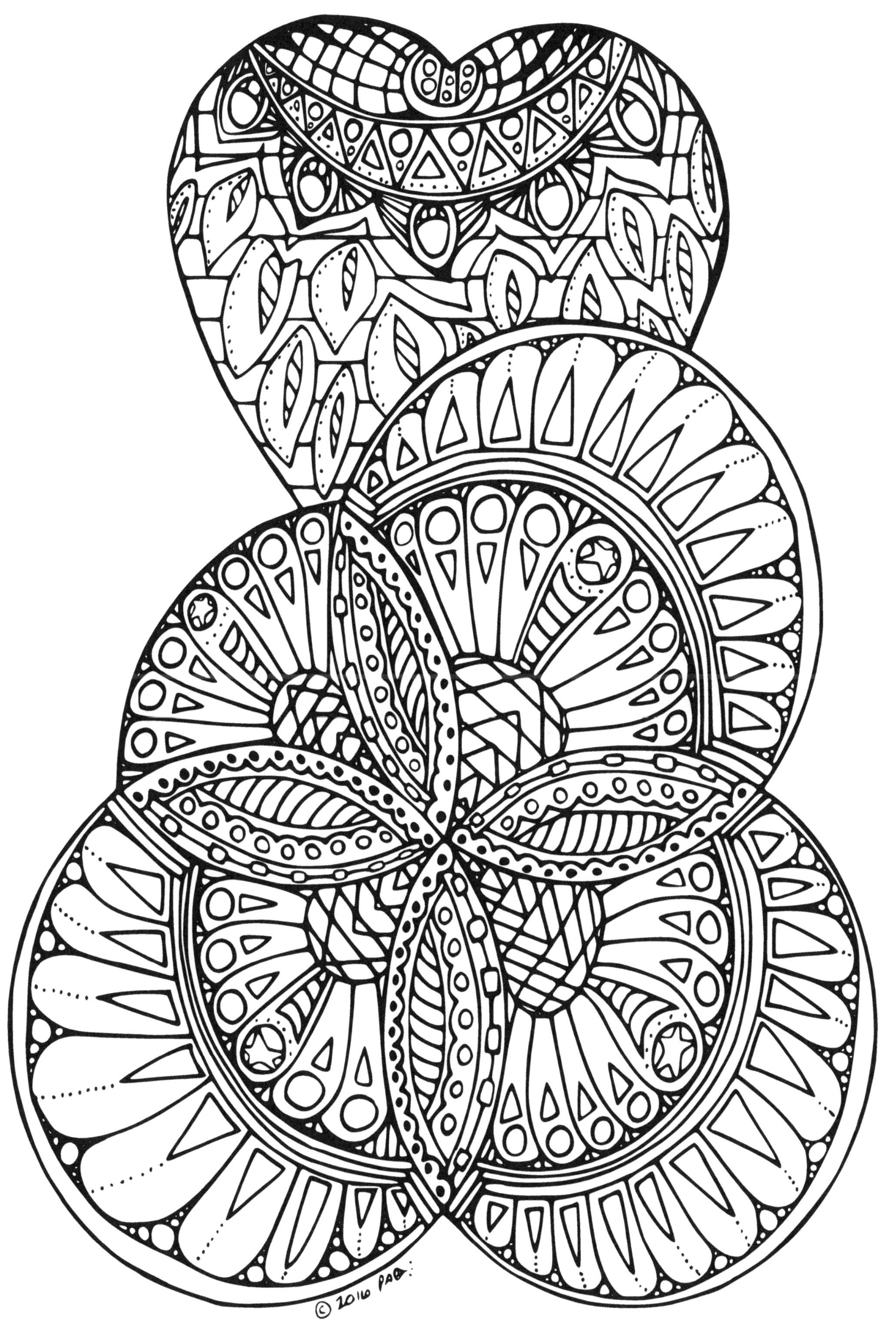
© 2016 PAB

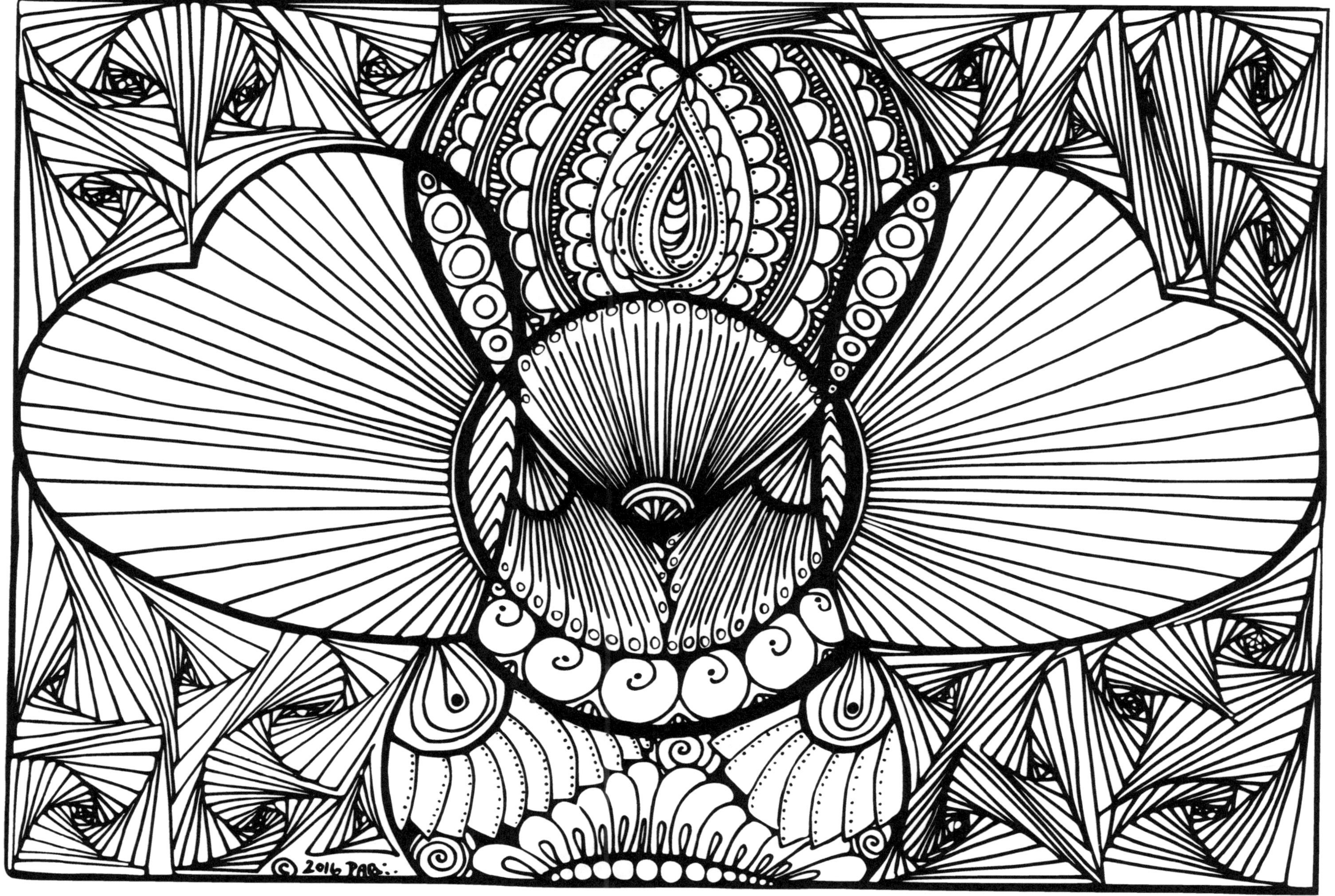
© 2016 DAB

www.ingramcontent.com/pod-product-compliance
Lightning Source LLC
LaVergne TN
LVHW081421110826
845149LV00010B/1818
9780997595932